INTEGRATION: THE P CO-ACTIVE IN WO1

Ann and Karen, thank you for this wonderful example of integration, the hallmark of a healthy brain and the guiding principle for healthy relationships, workplaces, and communities. Because you incorporate your own personal experiences, we readers don't have to set aside our human interest in order to benefit from the neuroscience. Karen's experience in developing Co-Active Coaching, a cornerstone of coaching practice, and Ann's ability to put brain research into practice incorporate both "what to do" and "how it works." This is integration at its best: stimulation for our thinking, doing AND being to make a difference in the world.

Linda J. Page, Ph.D., President of Adler Coaching and co-author (with David Rock) of *Coaching with the Brain in Mind*

An important book, filled with clarity and insight, which diagnoses separation as the essential malady human beings suffer from, and offers a practical and detailed path beyond it, towards harmony and wholeness.

Steve Taylor, Ph.D., author of *Back to Sanity* and *The Fall*

We have worked very closely with both Karen and Ann for a number of years now and have seen firsthand the tremendous impact they have had on both the coaching profession and the clients of the coaches who utilize their insights.

Karen has had a profound impact on the coaching industry, driving the coaching industry forward since early on in its inception and Ann's work on neuroscience is very much at the cutting edge. The book *Integration* draws deeply on their expertise and offers very practical tools, which can be used in

both a business and life context. They effectively and persuasively explore current scientific research that illustrates how using the Co-Active Model will lead to both a more integrated work and life. The book delves deep into the Co-Active model and readers really gain a sense of the power of the model. Bravo to Ann and Karen for super insights from two true masters.
Ben Croft, President, World Business and Executive Coach Summit

Betz and Kimsey-House extend CTI's pioneering Co-Active work into the deeply personal and urgent human question of how we become more fully ourselves while joining with others in creative relationship. Business and personal examples abound, as do tools and tips for application to development. Drawing from wellsprings as diverse as neuroscience, evolution, and developmental psychology, this book on integration is in itself a work of integration.
Doug Silsbee, author, *Presence-Based Coaching*

Integration is outrageously compelling. Betz and Kimsey-House explore Co-Activity by inviting us to stand in the hyphen of connectivity. Interconnectedness, they show us, is both creative and neural, both/and, never either/or; whether tracing and exploring the vagus nerve and/or taking us into the simile of navigating life's chaotic waters as though responding to aquatic turbulences in a canoe, the authors teach us gently, simply, elegantly about living life transformatively.

Poignant real-life stories – inclusive of their own very vulnerable truths of experience – emerge from the authors' worlds of coaching and leadership. In the same vein of heart-connection, the book renders quotations that burst with meaning. Betz and Kimsey-House see humanity at the cusp of the Great Turning – an opportunity to step into the power of interconnectedness, away from the silos of existence to which we have become accustomed. Who do I and who do we want to be, they ask in so many different ways. Most importantly, they offer us a process for integration through learning about, trying out, and living from many aspects of the Co-Active Model, a solid footing from which to make the Great Turn. Early in the book, Betz and Kimsey-House express their fervent hope that readers find the book "intriguing, provocative, and inspiring" and I believe readers will find it just that and so much more.

Dr. Don Morrow, CPCC, PCC, Co-owner of The Monarch System™

Integration:
The Power of Being
Co-Active
in Work and Life

Integration:
The Power of Being
Co-Active
in Work and Life

Karen Kimsey-House and Ann Betz

CHANGE
MAKERS
BOOKS

Winchester, UK
Washington, USA

First published by Changemakers Books, 2015
Changemakers Books is an imprint of John Hunt Publishing Ltd., Laurel House, Station Approach,
Alresford, Hants, SO24 9JH, UK
office1@jhpbooks.net
www.johnhuntpublishing.com
www.changemakers-books.com

For distributor details and how to order please visit the 'Ordering' section on our website.

Text copyright: Karen Kimsey-House and Ann Betz 2014

ISBN: 978 1 78279 865 1
Library of Congress Control Number: 2014957341

A CIP catalogue record for this book is available from the British Library.

Design: Lee Nash

Printed and bound by CPI Group (UK) Ltd, Croydon, CR0 4YY, UK

We operate a distinctive and ethical publishing philosophy in all
areas of our business, from our global network of authors to
production and worldwide distribution.

CONTENTS

Integration

we're not
accustomed
to holding
both
the this
and the that

our internal rivers
overflow their banks
or dry up
completely
as we are
pulled wildly
to chaos
or bound tightly
by rigidity

some of us spread
our energy
out past
the shore
creating marshes
and murky swamps
losing the
propelling current
in our desire
to touch
everything
and avoid
constraint

others pull back
measuring
the flow
with numbers
and spreadsheets
certain it can
be understood
controlled
and mastered
never noticing
the pulsating rush
dwindling
as we go

but when we
tend our waters
carefully
providing enough
in the way of borders
to contain
their power
without
restricting
the leaping waves
that carry us
through a
passionate life

we flow
we dance
we soar

~Ann Betz

Ann's Story and Karen's Story

Ann's Story

When I was seventeen I lost my hair. I'd had an autoimmune disease called alopecia almost my whole life, with small circular bald spots appearing and disappearing in my thick hair since I was three, so at first I assumed the ever-increasing patches would fill back in like they always had. Except this time they didn't, and within about six months I was almost completely bald.

I had been a theater brat, loving the stage and the limelight since I'd starred in the sixth-grade Christmas play. I practically lived in the high school theater, took acting classes at a nearby college, and performed everything from Shakespeare to Anne Frank on local community stages. I was pretty and vivacious, and invariably cast as the ingénue. My dream was to study serious theater in college, and act in a reparatory company or even perform on Broadway.

That was, until I lost my hair and "knew" my dream was over. What's more, somehow it felt like I'd lost my full rights as a member of the human tribe. Now I know that sounds dramatic, but even now I recall so clearly how I felt at seventeen. I'd watch carefree people in TV commercials and feel that there was no room in that reality for me, a bald girl. I felt—ashamed. And oh, so separate.

I think it's possible that before losing my hair this separateness was lurking under the surface of my life. I was never as skinny as the Seventeen *models in their tube tops and short shorts (this was 1981), and I'd grown up knowing my parents had an open marriage which was certainly not the norm. But I went to an alternative high school where we were all a bit different, and basically felt I fit in as well as anyone most of the time. And yet, there was something so disconnecting for me in losing my hair, something so fundamentally shocking and strange and different, that for the first time I experienced a profound chasm between myself and "normal" people. The chasm of separation.*

As I began to realize my hair was not coming back any time soon, I started wearing scarves and then wigs (always hoping it was temporary, of course). I was mortified if anyone commented on my hair or asked me if I was wearing a wig, and that exuberant girl who loved being center stage faded into the background so she wouldn't be noticed. Of course, this made me feel even more separate and cut off, as I removed myself from situations where there was the possibility of connection for fear of being seen, and therefore judged as less than by others.

But some people got through anyway, and at the height of my feelings of isolation, a group of older friends adopted me. They must have seen the spark alive somewhere inside me. They encouraged me to talk about losing my hair, and they brought me to personal growth seminars (it was the 80s, after all), where I saw with fascination that I wasn't alone in feeling alone. At age eighteen, I saw and understood it was part of the human condition to long to be part of the tribe, and to believe there is something shameful or wrong in oneself that is preventing this sense of belonging. For me, it was losing my hair. For others, it was addiction, or lack of success, or being from another country. I saw that it wasn't personal; I was somehow part of a general condition of aloneness. This realization was my own path home to myself.

It's over thirty years now since I was that young girl feeling so completely lost and alone, and I've come to see that losing my hair has truly been one of the most profound blessings of my life. One thing it taught me was the visceral understanding of what it feels like to step fully into the question that haunts us all—am I a part of things? On a basic, fundamental human level, do I belong?

Karen's Story

When I was eleven, my mother told me that she was ashamed of me. We had gone swimming at the community pool and after we got home, she took me aside. I looked so pretty, she said, when I came up from under the water, with my tanned skin and the water sliding off my dark eyelashes. But when I got out of the pool and began to walk toward her, she was embarrassed, she said, for people to know I was her little girl. I can still remember the flush of shame, from my toes to the tips of my blond hair. I wished for the floor to open up and swallow me.

Looking back, I wasn't really overweight. I was stocky and strong and far from the idealized, "perfect" girl that my mother wanted me to be, the one we always saw in magazines and on TV. Those girls were willowy and thin, or cute and bouncy like cheerleaders. They seemed to move effortlessly through life.

I was an intense adolescent, dramatic, angry, and lonely. I longed to be easy, to flirt effortlessly, and to giggle and laugh. I longed to be friendly and outgoing. If I had the chance, I probably would have given a limb in exchange for being one of the "really popular girls."

Instead, I felt awkward and shy, alone and afraid. I had boyfriends, but I never really felt like I belonged anywhere. Of course, I was constantly surrounded by images that reinforced my feeling of being all wrong. My shoulders were too broad. My arms were too short. My skin was not smooth enough. My hair was too straight and too thin. I was too big, too clunky, neither cute, nor graceful, nor beautiful.

My first year of college I was in the common area of my dorm when I overheard some girls talking about eating and then making themselves throw up. They were laughing about how much ice cream they could eat and how it was a surefire way to lose weight. The next day, I tried it on my own. And thus began twelve long years as a closet bulimic.

Actually "closet" is an unnecessary modifier. Being a bulimic and secrecy go hand in hand. Secrecy is one of the things that keeps the behavior in place. The other is shame.

I tried to stop many times over the years. I'd promise myself that I was going to stop. I would for a while, and then something would happen that was emotionally challenging and the cycle would begin all over again. Finally, I found myself at a dead end. I was beginning to have health problems. My life was going nowhere very fast. Then I saw a sign on a bulletin board at a local store for a group meeting of women with eating disorders.

I wrote down the address, and for several weeks in a row, I just casually walked by on the night the meetings were held. I was afraid to go in because then everyone would KNOW that I was a woman with an eating disorder, you see.

Finally, one night I got the courage to walk through the door. And the path home to myself began. The rest wasn't easy by any stretch of the imagination. There were times when I thought I wouldn't make it, but with the support of others managed to stay on my recovery path. In many ways, my battle with bulimia was my salvation. The physical challenge illuminated my path toward wholeness. I believe we each have our own challenges, our own "break in belonging," and our own path of healing. It's part of both the gift and the challenge of being a human being.

Introduction

Never underestimate the pain of a person, because in all honesty, everyone hurts. Some just hide it better than others.
~Will Smith

While these are our individual stories, we want to share them with you because we know they are also universal stories. Most of us struggle with various feelings of separation. For some (like the two of us) this comes from early incidents that make it clear we're not like everyone else. For others, it may be the inability to really succeed in a job despite best efforts, or the lack of intimacy in close relationships. A few, like our friend Max, live golden childhoods, excelling at everything, only to reach a "dark night of the soul" later in life, plagued by unexplainable anxiety attacks and fear they are not living up to early promise. Again and again, we find ourselves separate from ourselves, each other, even the world at large.

And yet, even within this sense of separation, it is becoming clearer that as humanity we are facing what Joanna Macy calls "the Great Turning." There is a heartfelt longing to find true connection, to make the shift from isolation and industrialization to a more holistic and life-sustaining society, one where instead of everyone being out for themselves, we experience the power of our interrelatedness. But in order to make such a turn, we need to understand not only where we are headed, but also where we have come from, and why.

We chose to write this book so that we could explore our fundamental disconnect, see the purpose it plays in the bigger picture of who we are as human beings, and offer both insights and solutions for transformation. We hope to be a positive voice in the crucial conversation about where humanity is heading — personally, communally and universally.

1

For us, Ann and Karen, there was a wonderful confluence of ideas that sparked this project, which are in themselves an example of integration. First, there is the powerful work of coaching in the world, now a well-established 25-year-old profession. In this area, Karen's work as the co-founder of and Ann's experience as a leader for The Coaches Training Institute (CTI) has shown us that the conversation about coaching has become much bigger than one-to-one support. People who have been exposed to the CTI model consistently report using ideas, concepts, tools and structures not only in their formal coaching relationships, but informally in their lives as well, achieving powerful, positive results. Again and again we hear, "CTI has transformed my life!" And so we knew it was time to make this information more widely available and accessible, beyond the people we encountered in coach training.

In addition, the emerging field of the neuroscience of leadership is showing more and more scientific underpinnings for human transformation, as well as direct connections to the effectiveness of coaching. Instead of saying, "you'll just have to trust me on this," science—and neuroscience in particular—is enabling us to make self-awareness, personal growth, and leadership development more accessible and real than was ever possible before, by building a bridge between the effective tools of coaching and the rational brain. This opens the door to personal and interpersonal integration, leading to a more solid, sustainable and heart-centered world.

What to Expect/How to Use This Book

The first part of this book explores our sense of separateness, of disconnection, and how it came to be. The second part provides stories and practical ideas for increasing transformative connection—what we call integration—in every area of life, including within ourselves. We base this part on aspects of what we call the Co-Active Model, the theoretical framework that

Chapter One

Separation

In truth there is but one problem and therefore only one answer...
the root problem is separation.
~Peter Erbe

The Human Story

We chose to introduce this book with our personal stories not to garner sympathy or set ourselves apart in our suffering, but because they serve to illustrate the larger human story. As leaders in the coaching field, we've both taught and trained all over the world, hearing life stories from many people across many cultures. The essence of the stories is the same—do I belong? Am I good enough? Am I a part of things? The experience of separation and the fear of not belonging is universal, and it affects us in every area of our lives.

This sense of separateness affects our professional careers, our family life and has a profound impact on every relationship we have. In this chapter, we'll explore the many ways we experience separateness as human beings—from ourselves, from each other, from life and nature, and from however we choose to define and inhabit our spiritual lives.

Separation from Self

For most, life is a search for the proper manila envelope in which to
get oneself filed.
~Clifton Fadiman

It's heartbreakingly common to feel separate from oneself, not fully knowing our own passions and preferences, living lives out of synch with our natures and misaligned from a sense of true purpose. Even pondering the question "why am I here?" takes a fair amount of courage, and thus is not something many of us do in our day-to-day lives.

It's interesting to note that a recent study found human beings feel the unease known as "existential angst" in the same area of the brain associated with both physical pain and the pain of social rejection. It's painful and distressing to ponder the meaning—or *meaninglessness*—we fear is inherent in our lives, and thus most of us generally avoid it, staying separate from ourselves, never really knowing our own core.

We come by this honestly, as most societies encourage a "go along to get along" approach to life, rewarding those who fit in and punishing those who don't. Modern public schools as we know them were designed to create workers who are ready to fit into existing systems, and even to this day far too often prefer to have children sit in rows without asking too many questions.

Karen knows the impact of needing to fit in and please. Growing up as the eldest of three in a military family, she learned to help out, stand up straight, and appear neat, pressed, and well behaved at all times, meanwhile never developing the capacity to know what she wanted and needed herself. "The summer I was seventeen, I was deciding where to apply to college. I wasn't sure whether I wanted to go to a large campus with lots of people and activities, or somewhere more intimate, quiet and small. And as I thought about it, I realized that, not only did I not know, I had no idea where to look to find out. I had no tools for understanding or knowing what I, from *inside myself*, truly preferred."

Karen's dilemma illustrates a common human problem: when we are encouraged (or required) to focus our efforts on getting along and fitting in, how do we determine what we ourselves want? And if we don't know what we want, how do we ever know who we are? And if we don't know what we want or who we are, how do we contribute our unique value to the world?

Survey, of all of our daily leisure time (about five-and-a-half hours on average), we only spend about forty-five minutes socializing. The rest is largely television and Internet use. In North America, the United Kingdom, and India, for example, studies show that the average parent spends between seven and eleven minutes a day talking with their children. Another UK study by the insurance company esure found that couples spend, on average, a little over three-and-a-half hours a week together, an hour-and-a-half of which is spent doing chores or in silence in front of the TV.

And even when we do connect with people we care about, all too often it ends up being a sort of "news report" or running commentary on our lives. "I did this, I went here, I crossed these items off my to-do list." Then we listen in turn to their report, and call it "catching up." What are we were actually catching up on? In the small amount of time we even talk to each other every day, how much do we actually *communicate*?

At the risk of stating the obvious, research by Dr. Matthias Mehl of the University of Arizona (among others) finds people seem to be happier when they spend more of their day having deep discussions and less time engaging in small talk. Authentically connecting truly does matter.

Deep connection brings us beyond the story and details of life. It requires that we stop and realize there is a human someone over there to be known and understood, not just a role or a title. While this sounds obvious, it's become the norm (especially Western society) to bulldoze through every day, moving from one item on the to-do list to the next. How many meetings start with an honest, authentic, personal check-in? How much of the time do we feel the pressure to "get down to business," forgetting that the person in front of us or on the phone is first and foremost a human being?

Ann was talking to a friend about this recently, who said, "What's really sad is that we aren't even very aware that we don't know each other. We base so much of our interactions on assumptions. I wish someone would say to me, 'You know what? I don't really know you.' Now *that* would be refreshing."

And yet, we come by this honestly, not because we are bad people. Our brains themselves are designed in part to interact with assumptions and prior beliefs. It takes a fair amount of the brain's energy to assess each situation anew as we move through life, which is not very efficient. Thus, we are designed to default to seeing what we expect to see and operating in habitual ways in order to save available brain energy for processing and assessment when it is deemed necessary. In other words, it simply takes less energy to assume people are their titles, reputations, and even stereotypes. And at the pace we're going these days, who has time to stop and ask, "Who are you, *really*?"

We used to inhabit societal structures that by their very nature connected us—our tribe, our church, temple or mosque, our family, our community. As we've become more sophisticated and moved into an increasingly global society, we've found new ways to interact (e-mailing, texting, etc) but not to *connect*.

Karen was recently having a conversation with a friend about upcoming local elections. "You know what?" the friend said. "One guy knocked on my door and introduced himself, and I found myself tempted to vote for him just because I had had the chance to connect with a real, live human being. I know it's silly, because of course his policy stance and voting record are much more important rationally, but for a minute there, all I could feel was the relief of actually meeting someone rather than looking at a postcard or an e-mail."

Separation from Life

Most people are on the world, not in it—have no conscious sympathy or relationship to anything about them—undiffused, separate, and rigidly alone like marbles of polished stone, touching but separate.
~John Muir

Many of us consume food that comes in packages. We don't plant, kill or gather it. We live in air-conditioned and heated homes, drive climate-controlled cars, and during certain seasons work from dawn to dusk, going days without being outside in daylight. Fear of abduction (or worse) has us keep our children inside or in supervised activities. The Internet has made it possible to get anything you want and visit anywhere in the world virtually (or create whole new worlds and new selves). Why go anywhere?

In Western society in particular, we've become separate from the pounding beat of life itself, and often feel like we have lost our place in the family of things. We are experts at control, taking food production to horrifying Frankenstein-like levels with genetically modified crops and factory farming. Our homes are pest-free and we sanitize grocery cart handles to prevent coming into contact with something that might hurt us. Sometimes it seems like if we could encase our children in plastic to prevent illness or injury, we would!

Of course, this is a scenario painted with broad strokes, and certainly isn't the case for everyone. Many people make conscious and even heroic efforts to stay connected to their food and the natural world. But it can feel like an uphill battle. While it's possible to live a life that is more connected to the earth, it takes a fair amount of awareness, effort, and intention to do so. In most communities and social groups, it's just not the default position.

When it comes to food, many nutrition experts today agree that the best way to shop at the grocery store is "around the edges." That is, avoid the center aisles with their processed and prepared foods. But even then, there is more and more concern that the fruits and vegetables, meats and milk we are eating, unless organic and not genetically modified, may be slowly poisoning us. For example, results from a German study published in the journal *Ithaka* found that people who have no direct contact with agriculture have significant concentrations of glyphosate (five to twenty times the permissible upper limit for glyphosate in German drinking water) in their urine. Glyphosate is the active ingredient in many broad-spectrum herbicides, including Roundup, and has been linked to a wide range of health concerns, including endocrine disruption, DNA damage, and birth defects in chicken and frog embryos. What's notable here is that these weren't people living on or near farms or dealing with herbicides in any way. These were city dwellers.

In other areas of life, in addition to the environmental ravages of our air and water, scientists have started becoming more and more concerned about noise and light pollution. In most major cities it's impossible to see the stars or have a truly quiet moment without the rumble of traffic or the roar of a neighbor's leaf blower. And this has an impact beyond mere annoyance. In a 2010 *Scientific American* "Ask the Brains" column, Mark Andrews wrote, "Stress resulting from background noise may decrease higher brain function, impairing learning and memory." Other studies have found that continuous background noise—all too common in today's households—has a negative impact on an infant's developing brain.

In contrast, Karen recalls the experience of being by herself on a meditation retreat. "I found a quiet spot up on a bluff with an amazing view of the valley below me, and I sat. I sat still and just felt the world around me, and the longer I sat, the more life I felt *in* me, as if I were integrally a part of things and connected to the energy of this beautiful world. It was such a different feeling than how I normally go through my day. I've tried to bring it in consciously since, but it's easy to forget."

Another example came from a friend who recently returned from a long-anticipated trip to Spain, who was telling Ann about her adventures. "It was—good," she said. "But not great. I realized that I sort of spent the trip looking through the viewfinder of my camera trying somehow to 'get' it all. We were so busy and concerned about seeing everything that there was no time for creativity. Now I realize that the most fun times were when we didn't have plans and just let ourselves explore." She saw Spain, but she didn't fully *experience* it. When we are so busy trying to check things off on a list or take yet another picture "to remember it by" we run the risk of missing the essence and connecting to life.

We spent thousands and thousands of years sleeping under the stars, listening to the wind in the trees, drinking from clear flowing streams, and eating food grown without hormones or chemicals. Of course we miss this, and on a primal level long for it in our very blood and bones. How could we not feel sad at our separateness from life itself?

Ann remembers the four years she and her family lived in Costa Rica. "Our house was quite open and the jungle just came in as it liked. After a while we got used to the various aspects of nature that wanted to come through the house, from army ants to the occasional tarantula. In all honesty, I didn't love the bugs, but when the hummingbirds stopped by to say hello or when we could smell night blooming flowers on the breeze, it kind of made up for it. I miss this feeling of being a part of things in that very visceral way."

Separation from God, Spirit, Universal Energy, Oneness

Most human beings imagine themselves to be separate from God. Out of this idea, humans imagine themselves to be separate from each other as well. Yet no human is separate from God, since God is Everything That Is. Therefore humans are not, and cannot be, separate from each other.
~Neale Donald Walsch

Perhaps at its very base, our collective experience of separation ultimately comes from the same source—our separation from

God (or whatever you know as oneness, source, the ultimate energy). The French theologian Teilhard de Chardin wrote that we are "spiritual beings having a human experience." Many traditions and teachers believe that at its spiritual core, this "human experience" is the illusion of separation from source. Enlightenment, then, is the experience of reconnecting to oneness and realizing the illusion while here on earth in human form. In this view, life as we know it is a journey back to wholeness, which is the truth of who we are.

In this book, we're not attempting to make an argument for the existence or nonexistence of God, but we do want to include this aspect of separation. It's a perspective that can help make sense of every other aspect of our feelings of disconnection. If we are here to experience the illusion of separation from all that is, then of course we don't feel connected to ourselves, each other, and the natural world.

The spiritual teacher Neale Donald Walsch makes the point that separation is important, a concept that allows for the whole to understand it is the sum of its parts. It's an interesting paradox. In this view, we are each separate, individual, and yet part of the whole. We are unique and different, and yet ultimately part of universal energy. We are each an individual manifestation of an ultimate wholeness longing to return to that wholeness.

In the next chapter, we'll further explore this idea as we look at how we got to where we are. For now, it's important to note that this feeling of being separate at the most profound level is an inherently human experience, from which all our other experiences of separateness flow.

For thousands of years, humans have struggled to understand our relationship with the energy of the universe. While we ourselves believe we are all co-creators of our interconnected existence, it's not clear how to actually grasp and experience being a part of it all. There's just too much and we're too small and vulnerable.

Perhaps our sense of separation is a way of protecting ourselves from facing life in all its complexity. Pain happens, disappointment happens, death happens. If we don't hold ourselves as separate, if we are indeed "co-creators," we must be creating *that*, too. Co-creating what we like and admire and co-creating everything we judge and dislike. Even co-creating everything that scares us. How could this be? Perhaps it's easier to believe we are separate.

Just
sit there right now.
Don't do a thing. Just rest.
For your
separation from God
is the hardest work in this world.
~Hafiz

Chapter Two

How Did We Get Here?

If we can really understand the problem, the answer will come out of it, because the answer is not separate from the problem.
~Jiddu Krishnamurti

As we explored in the last chapter, the beginning of the twenty-first century finds many of us feeling disconnected, distracted and adrift. This raises a few questions: How on earth did we arrive at this place? Has it always been this way? Were there times we felt more connected to ourselves, to each other, and to life itself? And even, is there a purpose and a point to it all? These are the questions we think worth exploring, hoping as we do to somehow find within them, as Krishnamurti said, an answer.

The Evolutionary Perspective

Progress is the attraction that moves humanity.
~Marcus Garvey

How, indeed, did we arrive at this state? We think that perhaps on some level we came to it intentionally. That is, our current state isn't some terrible fault of humanity, but rather, an essential part of our collective evolution.

According to anthropologists, *Homo sapiens* originated in Africa some 200,000 years ago and from there began colonizing the planet, spreading to Eurasia and Oceania about 40,000 years ago, and reaching the Americas around 14,500 years ago. For almost all of this time, we lived as hunter-gatherers, banding together in small nomadic tribes. The seeds of the modern agricultural state were only planted roughly 10,000 years ago when we began to domesticate plants and animals and stay in one place.

In doing so, we made a major shift from living in expanded kin groups of ten to fifty (sometimes growing to a hundred plus when food was abundant) to creating villages with hundreds of people, towns with thousands, and eventually cities, now numbering well into the millions.

Here's a bit of context for these numbers. If we have been around in our current *Homo sapiens* form for 200,000 years and yet only lived in large groups for 10,000 years or less, then we've lived tribally for 190,000 years, or 95 percent of human history. In other words, for 95 percent of the time we have been what we know as human, we have worked, gathered, slept, eaten, played, and created in small circles of belonging.

In his 1987 essay, "The Worst Mistake in the History of the Human Race," Jared Diamond challenges the popular notion that adopting agriculture was a major step forward for humanity. Instead of the harsh conditions we might imagine, the truth is that contemporary hunter-gatherer tribes, such as the Kalahari Bushmen, have plenty of leisure time, sleep and rest quite a bit, and actually work less, and work less strenuously than neighboring farmers. A Bushman was once asked why he hadn't copied his neighbors by growing crops, and he replied, "Why should we, when there are so many mongongo nuts in the world?"

Diamond found compelling evidence that our hunter-gatherer ancestors were overall taller, healthier, and had longer lifespans than their farming heirs (skeletal records from hunter-gatherers of the Mediterranean show that the average height was 69 inches for men and 65 inches for women, heights that are taller than average for Greeks and Turks today). Their diet was tremendously varied, bringing in a wide variety of necessary nutrients and protecting them from starvation if one particular food became unavailable, as happened in the great Irish potato famine of 1740, where at least 1 million died and a million more left Ireland. Quality of life indicators such as time spent working (fourteen to nineteen hours per week for modern hunter-gatherers—significantly less than farmers or office workers) and spacing of children (four years apart for hunter-gatherers vs. yearly for farmers) show that our ideas of "progress" may not be at all what we have been led to believe.

Whatever your views on whether or not things have improved for humanity since we settled down and began growing crops and domesticating animals, we have certainly expanded our small circles past the point where it's possible to know, let alone connect, with everyone in our sphere of contact. In 2010, British anthropologist Robin Dunbar found we have a mental limit of about 150 people with whom we can maintain stable relationships. (Others have proposed it might go as high as double that, but Dunbar's research is so popular and widely accepted that 150 has become known as "Dunbar's Number.")

It seems that we simply can't know and connect with the often more than 150 or even 300 individuals who touch our lives both directly and indirectly. The layers of people we are connected to, whether in our workplace, our children's schools, our community, or our local, regional, and national governments, is astonishingly large. This is not the way it was for most of human history. We *knew* the people who impacted our lives.

So why did we gradually begin to move away from this state of being intimately connected with everyone around us? Was it simple practicality due to diminishing food sources? Was it a gradual—or even sudden—expansion of our prefrontal cortices, making it easier for us to grasp planning and long-term goals? Or was it something else?

It's tempting to romanticize our tribal history. The sense of belonging to a group, having a place, a role, and a seat at the fire is comforting. There is something powerful in the idea of all of us being in rhythm with the seasons and the beating heart of the world, connected to the wind and knowing the plants and animals by their medicine. Even in traditional indigenous cultures ancient wisdom is increasingly disappearing with each generation, and there is a part of our collective being that (rightly) mourns this and longs to return from whence we came.

And yet, perhaps what propelled us out of our tribal existence was actually a collective desire to expand and express ourselves. Being part of a tribe provides structure and connection, but when we breathe as one being, what happens to the pieces that don't fit in? A friend of ours who grew up in Japan (a society that, while it can't be described as tribal, is all about conformity and fitting in) told us she personally couldn't wait to get out of there, even as a young girl. "We have a Japanese saying, 'the nail that sticks up gets pounded down.' I knew when I was twelve years old I was a 'sticky-uppy' nail and I would never be happy in my own culture. So as soon as I could leave, I did."

Maybe it's because both of us identify as "sticky-uppy nails" ourselves, but we think it makes sense that the ones who wanted more, who saw what else was possible, may have moved us out of tribal existence onto the next rung of the ladder of conscious evolution.

Theories ranging from Abraham Maslow's hierarchy of needs to Spiral Dynamics (originated by psychology professor Clare Graves, a colleague of Maslow's) to Dr. David Hawkins' "Map of Human Consciousness™" provide a framework for under-standing the sweep of human history in terms of our psycho-spiritual development. In this view, we are not just evolving the ability to use tools and communicate, but rather our very consciousness, both individually and collectively. We pass through stages, fields, or "memes" on our way to self-actual-ization, each new level transcending and including the previous ones.

In this view, we needed to move out of tribal consciousness, perhaps leaving—for a time—the deep sense of belonging to each other and the world for the sake of knowing what is possible for humans. We had to venture into greater and greater separateness in order to see the edges of human achievement and knowledge. Rather than stay content with "this is all there is," maybe the ones who moved us forward asked "what else?"

Like the iconic bird, Jonathan Livingston Seagull, whose passion for perfecting flight and unwillingness to conform resulted in his ostracism from the flock, history is full of examples of those who pushed the bounds of knowledge despite loneliness and criticism. Being content doesn't evoke change; being restless does.

It's in our very brains to want stimulation and challenge. Interesting research on the prefrontal cortex (PFC), the seat of executive function in the brain (governing decision-making, empathy, goal direction, and much more), shows that it needs a delicate chemical balance in order to be at its best. Too much stress, and the PFC gets overloaded with chemicals known as "catecholamines," such as norepinephrine (the adrenalin of the brain) and dopamine. Too many of these chemicals make it hard to concentrate, think long-term, retrieve and create memories, connect with others, and delay gratification.

This makes sense, doesn't it? We've all had the experience of being "stressed out" and not thinking clearly. Now here's something really interesting. When we don't have enough stress or stimulation, our systems release too few of these chemicals, *and it has the same effect.* Yale professor Amy Arnsten likens the PFC to the fairy tale character Goldilocks, who rejected every-thing in the three bears' cabin as "too hot" or "too cold," "too hard" or "too soft" in her desire to find what was "just right." Our prefrontal cortex also needs to have everything *just right* in its chemical environment in order to function optimally. Too little or too much going on, and our highest brains simply aren't as focused or creative.

Trying something new, changing patterns, and following a

different path can be stressful. But this isn't all bad. Maybe those ancestors of ours who dared to try something new actually found more clarity and focus in their brains!

In his groundbreaking book, *The Master and His Emissary*, Iain McGilchrist looks at human evolution through another aspect of the brain: the different goals and desires of the right and left hemispheres. Through analyzing literally hundreds of current brain studies and also looking deeply into philosophy, anthropology, and the broad scope of human history, McGilchrist makes the persuasive case that we are meant to be right-hemisphere dominant, but have moved away from this over the past two to three thousand years.

McGilchrist argues that the most important thing about the two hemispheres is not so much what they *do*—in fact, there is little activity we engage in that does not tap both hemispheres in some way—but how they *experience the world*. The left hemisphere sees only representations of things. It engages with what it already knows, taking apart, organizing, and analyzing information. For this part of the brain, the world appears as particles and pieces to be examined and manipulated.

The right hemisphere, by contrast, sees things holistically and brings into our awareness that which is new and alive. Everything we newly experience comes in through its gateway. Life, meaning, connection, empathy, and most of our emotions are all the domain of the right hemisphere.

While the left hemisphere asks, "How does it work?" the right ponders, "What does it mean?" Our left hemisphere is what knows we are separate and distinct, our right hemisphere, perhaps not. In her fascinating book, *My Stroke of Insight*, Jill Bolte-Taylor describes one of the effects of a massive stroke in her left hemisphere: "My body was propped up against the shower wall and I found it odd that I could no longer clearly discern the physical boundaries of where I began and ended." As her left hemisphere becomes more impaired due to the stroke, she speaks eloquently of the constant "brain chatter" (largely devoted to details and to-do lists) ending in her brain, leaving her aware of herself as some form of pure consciousness, but unable to manage the smallest tasks of daily existence.

Clearly, as Bolte-Taylor and McGilchrist point out, both hemispheres are essential to our survival and effectiveness. The problem is, in the developed world we've evolved into largely more and more of a left-dominated society. We prize utility over meaning, and are so busy trying to make it "to the top" (or even just "make it") that we have lost much of what is essential and important as humans.

Consider the following illustration: During the aftermath of 2012's Hurricane Sandy, one of Ann's friends reported checking in on a New Jersey acquaintance in one of the hardest-hit areas of the storm. "Oh, don't worry about us," he e-mailed back to her. "We have a generator, ha ha. Sure feel sorry for those suckers who didn't plan ahead (not)!" Contrast this with the story of the anthropologist in Africa who was playing with some children and proposed a race to see who could get to some sweet fruit first. The children all held hands and ran together, then sat down to enjoy the treats. When the anthropologist asked why they did that, they replied, "How can one of us be happy if all of us are not?"

Unfortunately, stories like the one from New Jersey are all too common, even expected, but it is the contrasting examples that inspire us—and often tragedies do bring forth a wellspring of love and generosity as well as fear and selfishness. In moments of distress, some turn inward with selfish regard for themselves only, while others are motivated to help. Could it be that they are at different points on the evolutionary journey?

A powerful perspective on the trajectory of human development is that we went from wholeness, connectedness, and, if you will, right-hemisphere dominance, to separateness, differentiation, and the rule of the left hemisphere. This was not a fault or even a bad thing. It was a necessary part of the journey—we had to push beyond the bounds of tribe to discover who we are and can be.

The Spiritual Perspective

A human being is part of a whole, called by us the Universe, a part limited in time and space. He experiences himself, his thoughts and feelings, as something separated from the rest, a kind of optical delusion of his consciousness. This delusion is a kind of prison for us, restricting us to our personal desires and to affection for a few persons nearest us. Our task must be to free ourselves from this prison by widening our circles of compassion to embrace all living creatures and the whole of nature in its beauty.
~Albert Einstein

In addition to the human evolutionary perspective we've examined, there is another perspective worth exploring. We'll call it the spiritual oneness/illusion perspective, and it goes something like this:

1. All is one (ultimately). Some call this God. And since it seems to be the case that we all came from the same small amount of matter, which exploded in the Big Bang, then there is even a scientific basis for these claims.

2. Oneness cannot know itself. We need an edge, a distinction, in order to know anything. If everything is my hand, I can't see or know my hand. I need there to be not-hand in order to know my hand. By the presence of that which is not my hand, my hand comes into focus. The same applies to oneness, to God.

3. Oneness created the illusion of separation so that it could know itself. By seeing and experiencing that which is not oneness (this experience—or illusion—of separation we find ourselves in), oneness comes to know itself.

4. Thus, all separation is an illusion designed to help us come to greater awareness of that which we already are. We feel separate (it's part of the game), but really, we're not. We can't be. We're just facets of the diamond of consciousness, experiencing different ways to be.

5. In this view, life (or if you believe in reincarnation, lives) is nothing more than a journey through a dream. Our ultimate reality is interconnectedness. Our true selves are whole and a part of everything.

This perspective isn't the sole provenance of a particular religion. (In fact, some religions would agree with it, while others most emphatically would not.) However, many spiritual teachers from different faith traditions have pointed to this view in their writings and teachings. From Jalāl ad-Dīn Muhammad Rūmī, the thirteenth century Sufi poet usually known as simply "Rumi," who wrote, "I belong to the Beloved, have seen the two worlds as One," to St. Thomas Aquinas, the thirteen century scholar widely regarded as the greatest Catholic theologian, who said, "God's arms then opened up and I entered Myself," the great religious mystics and thinkers point us again and again to our essential oneness with all that is.

In our natural state, we are glorious beings. In the world of illusion, we are lost and imprisoned, slaves to our appetites and our will to false power.
~Marianne Williamson

Now What?

And so, over about 10,000 years the individual gradually moved further away from the whole. On the human level, this meant finding identity beyond the tribe. On the spiritual level, knowing what it is to be an aspect of God. We spread out all over the globe exploring every nook and cranny, even sending emissaries as far as the moon. We have created innumerable religions, and used our beliefs to produce the ultimate in separation, the destruction of those not like "us."

In our quest to develop and know ourselves, we have gone as far out into space as we can, as far into the atom as possible, and as deep into the heart, the brain, and the soul as we can—ever questing further. We've discovered how fast a human can run, how high one can jump, how much one can remember, and we are ever pushing the edge of what one can know. This is our seeking, our differentiation from the tribe: we had to understand ourselves.

In knowing ourselves, we have also become as disconnected as we possibly can, pushing science to the point of not only being more and more efficient at killing one another, but, with the atom bomb, at wiping out whole cities and continents. It is said that when J. Robert Oppenheimer (the father of the atomic bomb) beheld the mushroom cloud test, he thought of the Hindu scripture: "Now I am become Death, the destroyer of worlds." Aloud, however, the physicist is reported to have made the ultimate engineer comment: "It worked."

As we stand in these early years of the 21st century, we are at risk of going as far as humanly possible in the direction of disconnection. We possess the knowledge and technology to actively destroy the world many times over through bombs or chemical warfare, not to mention what we are doing through global climate change, genetic modification of the food supply, and other scientific "advancements" we may come to deeply regret.

Although we of course haven't yet destroyed ourselves, the so-called "Doomsday Clock" maintained by the Board of Directors of the Bulletin of Atomic Scientists is currently set at 5 minutes to midnight. This clock, which symbolically estimates how close we are to global disaster, originated in 1947 to reflect the likelihood of nuclear war. According the Bulletin of Atomic

Scientists, since 2007 it has also included global climate change and "new developments in the life sciences that could inflict irrevocable harm."

Just as Darwin's finches adapted in beak size to more fully utilize available food, evolutionary leaps seem to require a crisis of some kind. Surely we are facing one of mammoth proportions now. The question we must address as humanity, with the clock set at five minutes to midnight, is now what? Who must we become? Will we, as Marianne Williamson puts it, stay lost in illusion, slave to the "will to false power?" Or will we step into the challenge we face, evolving to the next glorious phase of human awareness?

Chapter Three

Integration:
The next phase of human awareness

Integration enables us to be flexible and free; the lack of such connections promotes a life that is either rigid or chaotic, stuck and dull on the one hand or explosive and unpredictable on the other. With the connecting freedom of integration comes a sense of vitality and the ease of well-being.
~Dr. Daniel Siegel

What is the next phase of human evolution? The answer will not be found by returning to some idealized version of harmonious tribal life (even if we could), but neither does it live in further separation from each other, the world, and our very selves. We may have moved beyond the limitations of living as one, but where we have arrived today on the journey of human development now brings tremendous disconnection, causing loneliness, pain and disillusionment.

And so there is a pull to finding a place of belonging, which for some of us has meant getting lost in a group identity, dividing ourselves by religion, politics, ethnicity, and many other ways. While this can indeed provide a feeling of community, any sort of divisive us/them way of viewing the world is in reality a step backward in our evolution.

We believe that the way forward can be found instead on the path of *integration*. And by integration we mean, as neuroscientist Dr. Dan Siegel defines it, "the linkage of differentiated elements." The time has come to resolve the paradox, to move out of the "either/or" world we have lived in far too long. We must link again—our very souls require it—but as the unique, powerful, "differentiated" beings we were meant to be.

In this chapter we'll look at integration from a big picture perspective; in subsequent chapters we'll explore the many ways the philosophy, processes, and tools of the Co-Active model help us create integration with ourselves, each other, and our world.

What Is Integration?

There is one thing stronger than all the armies in the world, and that is an idea whose time has come.
~Victor Hugo

Integration feels very much like an idea whose time has come. We love Siegel's definition of integration as "the linkage of differentiated elements" because it provides the perfect road map to work from as we explore a tremendously powerful idea, one that we believe may even point us to a new chapter in our human story.

Linkage is the connection of separate components to one another. *Differentiation* is the process by which parts of a system become specialized, unique, and individualized in their growth and development. The next phase of human evolution is one in which we master integration—retaining our uniqueness while at the same time connecting at a deep and profound level with ourselves, each other, as communities, and with the generative power of the universe itself.

We have been socialized to believe in polarities, that we live in an "either/or" world, one which can be sorted and graded. We love to discuss and debate the value of various political systems, genders, neighborhoods, religions, lifestyles, or computer operating systems (just to name a few), endlessly arguing over which is better, hoping for some understandable and final ranking, some proof that our own opinion is best.

If we are artists, we may revel in an open flow of creativity and possibility, sometimes feeling disdainful of those we consider "too linear." If we are accountants or lawyers, we may enjoy our ability to make sense of things and put them in order, sometimes despairing of what we consider a woeful lack of focus and practicality exhibited by those we consider "too scattered" or "unrealistic."

In talking about the seductive nature of polarity thinking with some colleagues recently, one of them had this insight to share: "When I'm caught in it and can reflect back, I think there is a satisfaction that comes from the familiarity of choosing between two relatively known aspects, even if they are both unsatisfying, rather than opening up to all the possibilities of the unknown, which is where most of the magic happens. I have a sense that our little untrained brains typically see uncertainty as impending doom instead of greeting it with 'whoo hoo' and 'yippee!'"

As humans, we have long been at war both with each other and with ourselves, endlessly comparing our own views, habits, and beliefs to those of others, and in the process inevitably confronting a sense of deficiency, be it in ourselves or the other. Integration, on the other hand, says there is room for both sides in any polarity, if we let go of needing to make one aspect right or better, and the other wrong or worse. Integration points us to finding the value in every part of ourselves and each other, especially as we grow, develop and change.

One of our friends, an artist and a coach, recently began studying the brain. "I never liked my logical side before this," he said. "I thought if I paid attention to it I would lose my creativity and inspiration. I realized I was holding it as an either/or thing. Now I see I can use both—in fact that I am always using both— and the key is not one or the other, but flowing back and forth with ease. I have a huge new respect for my whole brain now!"

Integration calls us to stand comfortably in paradox. To know and value each part of a system, and also continually work to link the parts together.

Linkage

Only connect! That was the whole of her sermon. Only connect the prose and the passion, and both will be exalted, and human love will be seen at its height. Live in fragments no longer.
~EM Forster

As we explored previously, for much of human history, we were profoundly linked in small kin groups—perhaps, in the earliest times, even moving and knowing as one entity, like a flock of birds flowing through the sky together, or a school of fish evading a predator. We still carry this tribal knowing of each other within us as protection and connection on the most basic level.

For example, we can, like dogs, smell fear (although we are generally not consciously aware we are doing so), and our own bodies respond as if we ourselves are afraid. Studies ranging from the US Department of Defense to the University of the Netherlands have found that we react to fear-induced sweat differently than exercise-induced sweat, even when it is not possible to actively identify a difference in odor. In the case of fear (the most measured, although some studies have also looked at disgust and other emotions), fMRI scans show increased amygdala activation in non-threatened volunteer "sniffers" of stress-induced sweat in one study, and saliva taken from the volunteer sniffers in another study showed increased adrenalin and cortisol, both of which are markers of stress. Through smell, our own bodies experience the emotions of those around us.

There is also significant research on what are called "mirror neurons," which point to this fundamental ability to know and feel each other as well. A mirror neuron is one that fires both when an animal acts and when the animal observes the same action performed by another. Thus, the neuron "mirrors" the behavior of the other, as though the observer were itself acting. Many researchers argue that mirror neurons may be important for understanding the actions of other people, and for learning new skills by imitation. Mirror neuron systems in the human brain may help us understand the actions and intentions of other people and may serve as the neural basis of the human capacity for emotions such as empathy.

This area of study is very new in the field of neuroscience, and thus what mirror neurons can and cannot do is still the subject of much research and debate. The question of how and why we respond in synch with one another is fascinating, and there is certainly more to be discovered.

But even if it turns out that mirror neurons are not responsible for empathy and our sense of feeling one another's feelings, we know that we also mirror each other physically in many subtle ways, and this impacts our own internal biochemistry. Psychological research shows we tend to (generally) unconsciously copy the body posture, tone, and even facial movements of those we feel connected to. And further research tells us that how we position our body creates its own chemical response. For example, if we are sitting with someone having a pleasant chat, we might put ourselves in similar relaxed postures, which signal a flow of chemicals associated with a peaceful state. If we are with someone who is angry, our own jaws and shoulders may tense in response, triggering stress chemicals in our own bodies.

Research by Amy Cuddy shows that when we take on what she calls "power positions," or positions of dominance, our bodies respond by producing more testosterone and less cortisol. This correlates with a slew of additional studies on such things as the impact of smiling to improve one's mood, and standing up straighter to improve confidence. The body will produce the internal state of the position we put it in. Thus, if we are unconsciously mirroring someone else, we will replicate their own internal state.

We are interconnected as humans not just through biology, but also by culture, language and the environment. As John

Donne said, "No man is an island entire of itself; every man is a piece of the continent, a part of the main..." And not only do we feel and smell and know each other whether we like it or not, we also long for a certain level of connection.

We carry with us the primal imprint of the circle around the fire, where safety was found in closeness with tribe and community. To our ancestors, the world was a dangerous place on one's own, where we faced threats unmanageable alone, but often conquerable as a group. Somewhere in our beings we still remember this time, even as modern-day society (especially in the West) has pushed us further and further apart.

We are linked, and we long to be linked, while at the same time knowing our separate value. So now the next phase of human evolution calls us to be *intentionally* linked as the amazing, unique differentiated beings we are. This takes self-awareness. If I know who I am, and respect who you are, I can link with you without either diminishing myself or taking over. If I don't know who I am and I don't respect who you are, there can't really be linkage.

Which brings us to the next aspect of integration.

Differentiation

It is not our differences that divide us. It is our inability to recognize, accept, and celebrate those differences.
~Audre Lorde

The desire to know ourselves may well have been a key factor in moving us forward in our human evolution. Under the definition of integration we are using (the linkage of differentiated elements), we'll call this desire to understand ourselves *differentiation*, which is again the process by which parts of a system become specialized, unique, and individualized in their growth and development.

Differentiation is key to being able to powerfully and effectively link with others and even with oneself. One of the many reasons the field of coaching has become so popular in the past twenty years is that it helps people explore, understand, and claim their particular uniqueness and gifts. As humans, we are beginning to understand the importance of self-awareness in regard to increasing effectiveness in every area of life. A powerful example can be found by examining most reputable executive leadership programs. It used to be common that these programs focused primarily on skills and knowledge, but now almost all inevitably begin with some form of self-awareness and/or values, style or strengths inventory.

We are moving away from the days of "one size fits all" management to an understanding that the best leaders are those who first and foremost know who they are and work to develop their own innate strengths rather than attempting to copy others. It's not radical any longer to say that there are many different— and equally effective—ways to lead, and that the most important thing is personal authenticity. This is another example of how we are evolving out of polarity thinking (the either/or paradigm)— leaders are seeing that they can be themselves *and* move things forward (as opposed to the old one size fits all model which basically said you had to be General MacArthur to get anything done).

It's also no coincidence that almost half of the Gallup organization's classic measures of employee engagement address issues directly related to personal uniqueness. This survey is used faithfully in companies around the world to gauge the degree to which employees have a positive or negative emotional attachment to their work, because research has shown that a workplace with employees who feel engaged and empowered is much more productive and has far less turnover than one with employees who are disengaged. Among others, the Gallup survey asks individuals to respond to the following statements:

- At work, I have the opportunity to do what I do best every day.
- My supervisor, or someone at work, seems to care about me as a person.
- There is someone at work who encourages my development.
- At work, my opinions seem to count.
- This last year, I have had opportunities at work to learn and grow.

Differentiation is key to the process of integration because linkage without differentiation restricts what is possible. Some people confuse the powerful sense of connection that linkage brings us with the need to have everyone be the same. That is, they believe that to be safe, we must be alike, and reject those who are not. But if we are all the same—or more accurately, are afraid to embrace our differences—we can't truly and powerfully link with others. Our fear of making waves, being different, or not fitting in actually robs us of the opportunity to authentically connect. If we are not being our true selves, warts and all, then connection is persona to persona, not being to being.

Some degree of friction and chaos is essential for transformation, but we often feel compelled to resolve conflict immediately or avoid it altogether. We tend to seek comfort and resolution and are not at ease standing in discomfort and the unknown, and yet, to differentiate ourselves, we must sometimes be willing to change, to explore new ideas and new behaviors, which is certainly not always comfortable!

Our human brains love to feel they know (and have control over) what is going to happen. According to Dr. David Rock, director of the NeuroLeadership Institute, one way of looking at the brain is to understand it as a pattern-recognition machine engaged in constantly trying to predict the near future. When we can't predict what will happen to us, it can lead to a lack of certainty, and this can feel like a threat, putting us into a classic "fight or flight" reaction. Fight or flight generates a biochemical state conducive to basic survival behaviors, but where we are significantly less able to access our higher brain and sophisticated reasoning abilities.

Change is uncomfortable and often uncertain, and yet, nothing evolves—not a person, a relationship, an organization or the entire human race—without the development of new patterns, new neural pathways. As Henry David Thoreau said almost two hundred years ago, "A single footstep will not make a path on the earth, so a single thought will not make a pathway in the mind. To make a deep physical path, we walk again and again. To make a deep mental path, we must think over and over the kind of thoughts we wish to dominate our lives."

To move to the next place of human evolution, we need to develop an ability to differentiate, which includes understanding that we are energy and energy must move. The truth is, we can't stand still. We are either growing or atrophying. There is no maintaining the status quo: as the saying goes, the past is an illusion and the future a fantasy.

Differentiation is also part of us in deep and important ways. As humans we have adapted to live on every continent on the globe. Our skin carries various pigments designed to react to light differently so that we can survive in both the African Sahara and the steppes of Russia. Our bodies come in a variety of sizes and shapes, and no two humans (except identical twins) carry the exact same fingerprints or DNA. In addition, culture, religion, language, and family systems shape us, as does every experience we have from our first breath to our last.

The human brain contains some 86 billion neurons, making potential neural connections as vast and varied as stars in the known universe. Even in the most homogenous communities, each person's particular experience will be somewhat different, and thus their brains will continually develop and respond differently.

There is a lovely and apropos line by Walt Whitman: "Do I

contradict myself? Very well then, I contradict myself. I am large, I contain multitudes." Of course we confuse, baffle, and contradict ourselves and each other in all our complex differences. We are large; we contain multitudes.

It's delightful that at the beginning of the twenty-first century it is more and more possible for people (at least in the Western world) to *choose* to do what they like for a living, to marry who they please, and to enjoy themselves in a myriad of ever-developing and changing ways. Marching out of step isn't the problem it once was. And with the advent of the Internet and global communication, finding a band that likes your particular step as well is not just a possibility, but almost a given. You like to dress up like the Wookie from *Star Wars*? There's a group for that. You enjoy discussing the finer points of horseshoes or Jenga? Yep, those groups exist too. Ideas spread almost instantly, so if you don't know if you'd like being part of a flash mob or could raise funds for charity as part of a naked calendar of middle-aged women, who knows, it may just come to your town for you to explore.

All of this is to say, we now more than ever have the power to know and express ourselves, instead of living disconnected, separate lives of what Emerson called "quiet desperation." This can bring us to a powerful new possibility for humanity— Integration. Instead of separation, we can now become integrated with ourselves, each other, the physical world, and even God.

Integration within Ourselves

If you bring forth what is within you, what you bring forth will save you. If you do not bring forth what is within you, what you do not bring forth will destroy you.
~Daniel Pinchbeck

Let's start with how we heal the separation within ourselves. All other aspects of integration begin here, with self-integration.

When we know who we truly are—both our light and dark sides, and have worked to find internal coherence—we are available to each other and the world. Carl Jung noted that enlightenment isn't about visualizing light, but instead comes from integrating the darker aspects of ourselves into our conscious personalities. The bigger we are, the more fully self-aware, the more there is to link with.

Not only do we need to understand ourselves much better (differentiation), we need to link the various aspects of who we are by integrating our own internal opposing forces, and addressing the pull between all of our internal polarities. The question isn't should I be this or should I be that? It is, instead, who am I with all my parts connected and communicating?

There is a very important part of our brains called the *corpus callosum*. It's a bundle of fibers that connects the right and left hemispheres, one internal linkage point of two key aspects of our being. According to researchers Juliana Bloom and George Hynd, its function is to facilitate the transfer of information between the hemispheres, as well as the inhibition of one hemisphere by the other. Both are important to our functioning and effectiveness as human beings. (Interestingly, according to a 2011 study at the UCLA brain-mapping center, one of the measureable differences found in the brains of long-term meditators is an increase in the size of the corpus callosum, as well as greater connectivity in other areas of the brain.)

While recent brain research has taught us that it isn't accurate to call people "right-brained" or "left-brained," as a state of being, it is the case that in most people, one hemisphere of the brain dominates at a time, depending on the function, task, or role we are playing. But in those who have embraced some form of mindfulness, functional magnetic resonance imaging (fMRI) scans show much more integrated activity during various tasks, as well as the inhibition of parts of the brain that may not be as helpful. (NOTE: In common language, we think of inhibition as restricting self-expression. For example, we say, "I wanted to dance at the wedding, but I was just too inhibited." However, here we are using the term in its simplest sense: to restrict or restrain, which can be a very helpful thing in the brain.)

In 2005, a number of Tibetan Buddhist monks submitted to fMRI scans as they practiced a form of meditation aimed at achieving a state of pure loving kindness toward all beings. The scans showed that for monks who had spent more than 10,000 hours in meditation, there were striking differences in brain function. Activity in what is called the "locus of joy," located in the left prefrontal cortex, overwhelmed activity in the "locus of anxiety," located in the right prefrontal cortex. One of the theories explaining this is that the more developed corpus callosum enables one hemisphere to stop activity in the other when it is not helpful to the current activity, thus enabling the monks to stay in a state of peace and contentment.

Let's look a little more deeply at what we need to integrate from both our hemispheres. To paraphrase brain expert Iain McGilchrist, it isn't so much what each hemisphere *does* that is important. Both are involved in language, creativity, planning, and taking action. There is little we do, feel, or think that doesn't activate both sides of our brain. What is important, however, is how they each view the world, and what each holds as most important.

Our left hemisphere is all about specifics. Some of the things it is responsible for include:

- Positivity
- Maintaining a clear focus and direction
- Analysis
- Logic
- The *symbols* of language
- Structure

The left hemisphere also has a tendency toward:

- Anger and blame
- Rigid thinking
- Seeing people as things, that is, in terms of their utility rather than their full selves
- Lack of awareness of emotional state (self and others)

The right hemisphere, on the other hand, is "responsible" for:

- Holistic view, seeing the big picture and the greater context—the *meaning* of language
- Empathy
- Inspiration
- Understanding music, poetry and metaphor

But also has a tendency toward:

- Pessimism, hopelessness, shame
- Emotional overwhelm, inability to recover from strong emotions
- Depression
- Fear and anxiety
- Inability to focus, sometimes inability to move
- Inability to put feelings into words
- Inability to move into action due to emotional overwhelm

Given these lists, it starts becoming clear that there is a need for both integration and inhibition. In the case of integration, for example, there is clearly a role for both symbols (left) *and* context (right) in using language and communicating effectively. When there is a right hemisphere deficit (such as in some cases of autism), the more subtle meanings can be lost and, in the extreme, even very smart people won't understand metaphoric language and will take things literally. The autistic character Max Braverman on TV's *Parenthood* portrays this well. He has learned to ask those around him if they mean things literally or if they are speaking in metaphor, so that he knows how to respond to what they are saying. As is common for some forms of autism, he understands the words exactly, but doesn't always appreciate the more subtle meaning behind them unless it is explained.

Conversely, with left hemisphere deficit or damage, the person may understand the meaning of things, but not be able to find the exact word for it, being frustrated in their ability to say what they feel. Interestingly, because music is largely a function of the right hemisphere, often stroke patients with certain left hemisphere damage can sing things they can't say! There is something about adding music to the mix that helps them find the words. That is, if you ask them to say the words to *Happy Birthday* they can't, but when asked to sing, they will be able to. The bottom line is, in most areas of life, we are constantly drawing on both sides of our brain.

In the case of inhibition, it also becomes more and more evident that to be optimally effective requires some ability of one hemisphere to inhibit the other, as was seen in the Tibetan monks, where the left hemisphere was able to inhibit aspects of pessimism in the right. By the way, that isn't the only shift observed in scans of long-term meditators—the right hemisphere in its turn seems able to inhibit the area of the left responsible for our feeling of separation, creating a sense of oneness and connection with all there is.

Differentiation *within* ourselves is actually critical to internal integration. We need to be aware of our own reactive tendencies as much as we need to know our "better selves." As mentioned above, the fight or flight response triggers a lower, less advanced part of our brain. This is often inaccurately referred to as the reptilian brain, but is actually the part that developed when we evolved into a mammalian state.

Many events can trigger a fight or flight response, from things that are truly dangerous to encounters we perceive as threats to our sense of status or control. When this lower part of our brain is activated, a biochemical response (largely a release of adrenalin and cortisol) occurs that is designed to help us survive in the moment. Energy goes to our extremities, making it easier to fight or flee, and is drawn away from more consumptive activities such as digestion or the immune system. And the brain goes into a state of hyper focus and reaction, dealing only with the threat (or perceived threat) in front of us, and is literally unable to access more complex thinking.

Often this is a subtle response, not the full-on actuality of truly fighting or running away that we might engage in were the trigger an actual threat. Instead, fight or flight can be activated by something as simple as an unpleasant e-mail or difficulty in traffic. And even a bit of the stress-induced chemical cocktail within makes balanced, effective decision-making more difficult.

In terms of integration, we believe a key aspect is being able to recognize (thus differentiating) our reactive selves, increasing the ability to link this part of the brain—our lower, animal/survival nature—with our higher, more thoughtful brain. Ann had a highly intelligent executive client who was very effective, except when he felt his status was threatened. Then he would send smart, sarcastic e-mails (a subtle form of "fight") without considering the consequences. His team and peers both respected and disliked him, because it often wasn't fun being on the receiving end of his communications, and he was finding his effectiveness as a team leader slipping without knowing why.

When Ann shared with him the brain science behind what he was doing—that, in effect, he was writing e-mails from a less-evolved part of his brain, it changed everything. He made a commitment to putting his snarky e-mails in a drafts folder before sending them, giving his brain a chance to calm down and assess whether this was really what he wanted to say. At one point, he slipped, telling Ann, "I sent another reactive e-mail the other day. My finger just pushed send before I could stop myself.

But this time, I knew I had done the wrong thing. It's going to take me the best part of a week to clean that all up! But at least now I know why I did it and I also know what to do to recover."

In essence, he is in the process of becoming more integrated, which doesn't happen overnight. What is encouraging is that his higher brain responded more quickly than it had in the past, telling him, "Uh-oh, look what we've done now." This is part of the path, and in making that mistake, he is one step closer to being able to inhibit, in the moment, his lower brain.

The paradox inherent within integration—the linkage of differentiated parts—is that as we differentiate and know who we are, we also become clearer about when we need to link things together and when we need to inhibit one aspect from taking over the whole show. The most effective, well-integrated people seem to be those who can easily access all parts of the brain as needed, as well as inhibiting the reactive aspects when they arise.

While there are many aspects of personal integration (Dan Siegel lists a full nine domains), we wanted to emphasize two to begin with: the different goals and desires of the two hemispheres and the need to be aware of and inhibit our lower, more reactive brain.

Integration with Others

I know there is strength in the differences between us. I know there is comfort in where we overlap.
~Ani DiFranco

In the popular book *Codependent No More*, author Melody Beattie introduced the general public to the idea that we can be overly involved with and even "addicted" to another person. She popularized the understanding that there are two extremes in relationships—independence and codependence. On the one hand, we can be distant, never letting anyone all the way in by maintaining an overzealous commitment to boundaries and personal space (extreme differentiation and separateness). On the other hand, we can lose our own identity in the other, working to please at all costs, even forgetting who we are in the process (extreme linkage). The concept of "interdependence" began to emerge then as a healthier ideal, and in this word we see the possibility of integration as we have been defining it: the linkage of differentiated parts.

In connecting with each other, the concept of integration as we are defining it is a powerful idea, whether it is with a significant other, a colleague, a child, a friend, one's workplace, or community. First of all, we need to be differentiated. If we don't know who we are, what we want, and what we personally have to contribute, the potential of any connection is diminished, and we run the risk of looking for our identity in the other or in the relationship itself. This can leave us vulnerable and disempowered, and devastated if and when it ends.

And secondly, we need to be able to link with each other, bending at times, learning, and being willing to be shaped and re-shaped by the experience of being related. To expand on this a bit, Dr. Daniel Siegel tells the story of asking thousands of people attending his lectures, from medical doctors to therapists, social workers and coaches, if they had ever been given a definition of the mind. An astonishingly small percentage of these people (almost all of whom worked intensely with people's minds) had ever had a class or even a discussion about what it is. So Dan set out to find out. He convened a cross-disciplinary group of academics from disciplines as varied as anthropology to neuroscience, and after a couple of years (yes, years) of conversations, they came up with this definition (one that they all could embrace in their own fields): *The mind is an embodied and relational process regulating the flow of energy and information.*

So what does it mean that the mind is relational? As we saw in the first part of this chapter, we feel and are affected by each other in ways we are not fully aware of. We are shaped by each other's moods, thoughts, and ideas, no matter how much we consider ourselves impermeable. And yet, we also have the ability to make conscious choices. We don't have to have the same prejudices as our families, for example. We can choose to be gregarious and open in a culture that is typically not. With practice, we can stop and breathe and open our hearts in the middle of an argument, even when our mirror neurons or subtle mirroring are reacting to the other person's anger or frustration.

When in relationship with others, integration calls us to link consciously. This means valuing ourselves as well as recognizing the gifts of others, being willing to be affected by them, and also aware of when it will be more productive to shift things in a more positive direction. In polarity thinking (viewing the world as either this *or* that, rather than this *and* that), differentiation means separateness, and linkage means losing ourselves. Integration gives us the awareness that both are not only possible, but deeply powerful and effective.

Integration with the World

Disorder is inherent in stability. True stability results when presumed order and presumed disorder are balanced. A truly stable system expects the unexpected, is prepared to be disrupted, waits to be transformed.
~Tom Robbins

All life flows between the opposing forces of chaos (the right hemisphere at its most extreme) and rigidity (the left at its most extreme). This is not a new concept. The great twentieth century philosopher and mathematician Bertrand Russell taught that all political systems calibrated to one of two forces: freedom or control. In the nineteenth century, the philosopher Friedrich Nietzsche argued that great dramatic arts were a unification of the energies embodied by the Greek gods Apollo (reason and order) and Dionysus (revelry, spontaneity, and enjoyment), energies once again reflective of rigidity and chaos. We are naturally pulled by these two powerful forces, and an effective life requires that we learn to dance with both.

Integration with life calls us to know, value, and link these seeming polarities, understanding that each is not something to be feared by the other, but rather exist as what Siegel calls "banks of the same river" — the river of our lives. We need the energy inherent in chaos to move things, and we need the energy inherent in rigidity to provide structure.

But many of us fear and resist one or the other of these energies, often embracing one side or the other in different circumstances and at different times in our lives, and rejecting the other in the process. At its most extreme, this can be like beaching your boat up on one bank of the river because you're so afraid of getting stuck on the other.

Ann remembers how ineffective a fear of rigidity was in her own life. "When I was seventeen I dropped out of high school. I couldn't see the rules and structure as anything less than a horrible restriction. I somehow managed to talk my way into college, but ended up going to five different schools before I finally completed my BA at age thirty. Each time it was the 'stupid rules' that got in my way. Finally, with a little maturity, I was able to see the rules and requirements as a part of the process — and possibly not even all bad! I ended up enjoying the required math and science classes I had dreaded and feeling very proud of myself for finally completing something."

On the other hand, we've both coached countless clients who find themselves at middle age, having followed all the rules and "shoulds" of life, now wondering what happened? Where is the joy, the zest, the fun? They did what they were supposed to do, creating safety and security for themselves and their families, only to realize one day that they may be living, but are not truly alive. They find themselves beached up on the dry shores of rigidity because they are terrified of chaos and its inherent uncertainty.

There is a pattern and a flow to life, both rules and chaos. As it says in Ecclesiastes, to everything there is a season, and a time for every purpose under the sun. To be integrated with life means finding the dynamic balance between enough structure and enough freedom so that things move forward powerfully. Too much structure, the flow is restricted and nothing can move. Too much freedom, and energy spills all over, without direction, and nothing gets accomplished.

It's fun to watch people canoeing or kayaking on a river. Novices often paddle hard on one side of the boat until they end up almost hitting the right bank, then paddle hard on the other side until they almost hit the left. But experts stay mostly in the middle, making micro-adjustments with each stroke. It looks like the boat is going straight—and it is—but it's not because it doesn't get pulled one way or the other almost all the time. The job of an expert paddler is to compensate, adjusting her stroke to the current, her fellow paddler, and the wind.

This is what being integrated with life calls us to do. To stay in the flow, ever honoring and adjusting to each bank of the river that supports us.

Integration with God, Oneness, the Universe

Since no one really knows anything about God, those who think they do are just troublemakers.
~Rabia of Basra (8th century female Islamic saint)

How can we even begin to talk about integration with God, oneness, the universe or spirit when none of us has any real idea what that is, much less any shared understanding across faiths and cultures? Any description we would give runs the risk of leaving someone out, and yet, there seems to be a universal longing that transcends any definition or label—the longing to feel a part of something larger than ourselves. To feel part of something without beginning, end, or limitation. To know ourselves, in Einstein's words, as a part of the whole.

So how do we integrate—link our differentiated selves—with something we don't understand? This is, for some of us, the ultimate journey of our lives. Pierre Teilhard de Chardin, as we previously mentioned, was the first to note that we are not human beings having a spiritual experience, but rather spiritual beings having a human experience. In the last chapter, we looked at the spiritual argument for separation, which boils down to oneness (or whatever you like to call it) desiring to know itself through the illusion of separateness—spiritual beings having a human experience indeed!

Differentiation and linkage operate here as well. In order to link with whatever we know as God or universal energy, we must first believe there is such a thing, and that it can be differentiated from what we know as ourselves. (The beloved Christian Saint Francis of Assisi wrote: "So precious is a person's faith in God, so precious; never should we harm that.") And it also requires that we stand in the most profound paradox of all— that we are both separate and inextricably part of everything. In our human experience, separate. On the spiritual level, one.

We asked a long-time spiritual teacher and friend what she thought about integration with God or oneness. "When I feel integrated with God," she replied, "I am not concerned about the past or the future. I am only aware of now. I have forgiven the things in the past I held as wrong, and I have no regrets. I am looking into the future without fear, trusting that all is well. In this sense, I don't just feel integrated with what I hold as God, I feel very integrated in myself as well."

In Conclusion

All things are difficult before they are easy.
~Thomas Fuller

Ultimately it all returns to integration with and within ourselves. There is a peace and power to knowing and honoring all aspects of ourselves: our mind, body, spirit, and emotions. Knowing and using (and inhibiting when necessary) all areas of our brain, and respecting our need for both structure and freedom. And from here, we can link our wonderful separate powerfully differentiated selves with others, with our communities and workplaces, and ultimately, with all there is.

We believe that the underpinnings, philosophy, tools and distinctions of the Co-Active model offer a much-needed road map for integration on every level. Originally created by Karen and her co-founders Henry Kimsey-House and Laura Whitworth to guide the coach training programs offered by CTI, the world's largest coaching and leadership development company, the Co-Active model is so much more than a methodology of coaching. In the following chapters, we'll explore how living a "Co-Active" life leads us to deep fulfillment, effectiveness, and connection with ourselves and each other.

Chapter Four

Being Co-Active

Boundary lines, of any type, are never found in the real world itself, but only in the imagination of the mapmakers.
~Ken Wilber

One reason we feel dis-integrated, separate, and fragmented is that we don't really know how not to be. We are bombarded with all too many examples and role models for a dis-integrated (and dysfunctional) life, from TV to politics to pop culture. We believe that by focusing on integration, on honoring our need for both separateness and linkage, is the true power of being Co-Active. To be Co-Active means not choosing between one polarity or another, but holding the complex dynamic tension of both.

In this chapter we will look more deeply into the nature and distinctions of "being Co-Active," as well as the many ways this philosophy creates integration in ourselves, with others, in community and with the process of life itself.

What Does It Mean To Be "Co-Active?"

Dictionary definition of Coactive: Coactive \ Co*ac"tive \ Adjective: Acting in concurrence; united in action.

Although CTI was founded in 1992, the actual Co-Active model was not created until founders Karen Kimsey-House, Henry Kimsey-House, and Laura Whitworth were seeking a way to describe their method of coaching for the first edition of *Co-Active Coaching*, published in 1995. Their writing collaborator, Phil Sandahl, literally looked through the dictionary to find the right word, and discovered the somewhat obscure term "co-active".

(The first noted usage of this word goes back to Shakespeare's *A Winter's Tale*: "With what's unreal thou *coactive* art...") The group decided it was the perfect term for the particular philosophy and manner in which they were training coaches, and thus CTI's coaching methodology became known as "Co-Active Coaching." As coaches brought forth the tools and distinctions of Co-Active coaching into the world, it soon became clear that being Co-Active was not simply a philosophy of coaching, but was also a road map for living a more fulfilled, integrated life.

The word Co-Active is an adjective, a way of being, an emergent and complicated stand one takes in the world, a word full of ambiguity and mystery. As an adjective, Co-Active does not exist somewhere you can point to (like a tree or a cloud), but rather emerges in relationship as a result of a certain way of our interacting with one another. Therefore, pinning it down is difficult to impossible. Just like love or freedom, we can only give examples of Co-Active. In other words, when we see a mother beaming at a child, we might be inclined to say, "Now *that's* love." But it's *not* actually love we are witnessing, because love isn't a thing. All we can honestly say is that it's one glorious beautiful *example* of love. The understanding is enriched by example.

For many years, the CTI founders resisted defining Co-Active, because once things are defined and set in stone, so to speak, it's human nature to be somewhat doctrinaire about them. The temptation is to make up lots of rules about what is and isn't right. They worried that people would try to put parameters around what *is* or *is not* Co-Active, as human beings are wont to do. This way of thinking, so deeply programmed within us, is actually the antithesis of what they were looking to model and bring forth in the world. The whole point of being Co-Active is to move away from the polarizing "either/or" perspective in which so many people find themselves stuck, and open themselves to the mysteries of complexity and possibility. The challenge of defining this term, however, has also allowed the Co-Active community to over the years explore and refine what it means.

We don't want to offer a list of dos and don'ts or rules for being Co-Active in this book, thus stifling creativity and exploration. Instead, we'd like to offer a sort of map of the Co-Active territory, while understanding ourselves that there remain areas as yet unexplored and undiscovered.

Why the Co? Why the Active? Why the hyphen? A view of the Brain

Dreams pass into the reality of action. From the actions stems the dream again; and this interdependence produces the highest form of living.
~Anais Nin

Perhaps the easiest and most elegant way to think about the two sides of Co-Active is that they are largely the categories of both unification/separateness as well as being/doing, and while both of these aspects may point to areas of brain research, it's important to understand that trying to actually pinpoint a concept like "Co-Active" in the brain is a challenging proposition. For one thing, it's not completely clear, even at this point in history with all our fancy technology, exactly what each part of our brain *does*. We can come close, but because it is a highly complex (and yes, messy) system, it's often difficult to fully understand the component parts. And just to make things even more challenging, there are also many specialized neural networks combining multiple areas, which are activated in certain brain states.

In thinking about the idea of being Co-Active from a brain perspective, it makes sense to us to look at both specific location as well as network activation in order to (perhaps) come closer to the whole picture. It's worth examining again the distinct role and purpose of the right and left hemispheres of the brain, and then also looking at the *default mode* and *task positive* networks, as both of these brain areas/systems have implications for our understanding of Co and Active.

The Right and Left Hemispheres

As we have discussed in earlier chapters, although each hemisphere is specialized as to function, neither operates as a brain unto itself. Rather, the two hemispheres integrate their activities to produce physical movements, mental processes and behaviors greater than, and different from, their individual contributions.

That being said, it's still true that our two hemispheres have specialized functions. These functions are important to understand because, as we have mentioned before, they point to a certain way of looking at the world. The right hemisphere gives us global awareness and a holistic view, while the left allows focus and specificity.

The corpus callosum connects the two hemispheres, playing a role not only in *linking* the two halves of the brain, but also *inhibiting* one or the other from dominating. Thus it is possible that a more integrated, "Co-Active" brain is able to link positive aspects of the hemispheres and inhibit negative ones. (This would correlate to research on long-term meditators, who are both shown to be more emotionally intelligent than average and also to have thicker corpora callosa as a result of meditative practices.)

The right hemisphere is more concerned with relationships, emotions, the big picture, meaning, purpose, and oneness, and has a softer, more inclusive way of looking at the world. Thus, we place it on the "CO" side of things, because this is the place we slow down and consider the greater impact on people, relationships, and the broader purpose. *(However, by placing it here, we don't mean to say that the right hemisphere has no connection whatsoever to action.)*

The left hemisphere is more concerned with logic, analysis and the sequential movement of things, and has a sharper, less inclusive (but more focused) way of looking at the world. Thus, we place it on the *active* side of things, because if ideas and possibilities cannot be broken down into component parts, it is not possible to move anything forward. *(However, by placing it here, we don't mean to say that the left hemisphere is inherently and solely concerned with action.)*

The right hemisphere (co) is where new things come into our awareness. The left (active) is where those things—recognized and brought in by the right hemisphere—take shape and form, and can be manipulated and worked with. We need the right, our co side, to bring in the possibility, and the left, our active side, to move into specifics (which can then move into action). When this is in place we find, as Anais Nin so rightly said, that we are called back to the dream, and then the action, and then the dream, and so on in an upward spiral of creativity.

Another way of looking at this might be that the co of Co-Active points to oneness, connection, and a holistic view of the world, a view held more by the right hemisphere of the brain. The active of Co-Active points to separateness, differentiation, and pulling something into focus so that it can be grasped and manipulated, the view of the world held more by the left hemisphere of the brain. Like a sculptor creating a work of art from stone, the active pulls out the potential that is there. But without the stone to create from, nothing would be possible. Thus the co, the pure being, the potential of everything, holds the active and gives it room to move, act, and create.

Despite lots of fun and entertaining online quizzes, research shows that no one is truly "right-brained" or "left-brained." However, it does seems that one hemisphere or the other can be over-activated in certain circumstances, such as when we are under stress, activating not only the positive aspects listed above, but also some of the more challenging ones such as hopelessness and emotional overwhelm for the right hemisphere, and blame, denial, and frustration for the left.

Thus, when we work towards being more Co-Active, we ideally help to create more balanced and effective brains in our clients (and ourselves), where we are able to use, as needed, the positive aspects of each hemisphere, without getting stuck in the negative states.

The Default Mode Network and the Task Positive Network

The Default Mode Network (DMN) and the Task Positive Network (TPN) are two distinct neural networks in the brain. The DMN is a network of brain regions that are active when the individual is not focused on the outside world and the brain is at wakeful rest. It's called "default" because it is the network that is activated *unless* we are specifically engaged in goal-directed activity, the realm of the TPN.

Probably one of the most interesting aspects of these two networks is that when the DMN is active, the TPN is not. And when the TPN is active, the DMN is not. Part of each network's function is to shut the other down.

The TPN deals with such things as focusing on tasks, actively paying attention (external), goal-orientation, reacting to and working with sensory information, short-term (working) memory, planning and abstract reasoning.

The DMN, on the other hand, is activated in dreaming, envisioning the future, long-term memory, gauging others' perspectives, theory of mind (understanding others), intro-spection, and self-referential thought.

Note: While some of the aspects listed may sound similar to Right and Left Hemisphere operations, each network actually includes both. Thus, adding an awareness of the DMN and TPN increases our understanding of what it is to be Co-Active.

Because the Default Mode Network is activated when we are daydreaming, imagining the future, pondering our own thoughts and beliefs, and trying to understand others, we place it on the Co side of things.

Because the Task Positive Network is activated when we are doing or focused on doing, we place it firmly on the Active side of things.

Perhaps even more than the right and left hemisphere, the DMN and TPN interaction helps explain why being Co-Active can be so challenging. When we are dreaming, reflecting, and standing in someone else's shoes, the neural network concerned with action is not "on line." And when we are planning and acting, the network associated with creating vision and understanding others is shut down.

By holding a Co-Active view, whether in terms of coaching, leadership, or life in general, we create a dance between these two networks. By holding focus on both the being and the doing, we can't help but create connections between the two networks, so that even if only one can be activated at a time, it becomes easier and easier turn on the switch of the other and shift back and forth more and more quickly.

In looking at the right and left hemispheres and the default mode and task positive networks, we can perhaps understand the scope and challenges of Co-Active a bit better. Ultimately, the true strength and brilliance of any person, whether they are a leader, parent, student, or coach, is not just the development of one aspect or another, but the continual commitment to inhabit this inherent paradox of the hyphen, increasingly honoring both.

The Philosophic View

Philosophers have debated the complexities of balance and integration for centuries: yin/yang, light and dark, masculine and feminine. The concepts behind the philosophy of Co-Active aren't new at all. In fact, being Co-Active might be more aptly described as a modern approach to ancient wisdom that has been largely lost in today's Western world, ruled as it is by Cartesian dualistic thinking.[1]

Instead of dualistic thinking, where the mind is profoundly separate from the rest of who we are, being Co-Active shows us that the world is fundamentally relational. In other words, while the Cartesian worldview that largely dominates today may admit the importance of both the "being" and "doing" energies, it does not see the full value of integrating them. In this classic (but limited) view, one that dominates the Western world today, while there is room for "this *or* that," the importance of this *and* that has not yet taken center stage. Now is the time!

Being relational means that the most important element of the descriptor Co-Active is not Co or Active, but in reality, the hyphen itself. What is crucial about Co-Active is not the power of being *or* doing, separateness *or* oneness, though arguments can and have been made for the past few centuries about the relative value of each, but the fact that the true magic of life lies in the integration of *both*. The wisdom of the ancients pointed us to balance and flow, to the deep paradox of holding yin *and* yang, to knowing both Apollo's calm rationality and Dionysus' spontaneity, to honoring masculine focus and feminine spaciousness, to finding, above all, integration in all things.

Being Co-Active helps us understand and make real the process of this integration. We start with the being, the meaning, the purpose, and the point, and make our lives real by moving into action from there. This is powerful everywhere—in our relationship with ourselves, in our relationships with all others in our lives, and in our relationship with life itself. Being Co-Active points us to honoring both the being and the doing at every moment in life.

Standing on the Hyphen

When I know I am nothing; that is wisdom
When I know I am everything; that is love
My life moves between the two.
~Nisargadatta

Being Co-Active points to the challenge of both being fully ourselves *and* linked with others powerfully. Popular wisdom tells us we have to compromise, sacrifice, and make concessions in order to get along. Most people are working on a polarity continuum between selfishness and codependency, or, to put it another way, between being fully self-expressed or responsible for their impact. On the one side of this polarity are those who are fully self-expressed, standing tall as individuals, not caring whether or not people like them or whether they get anything done. On the other side are those who are so concerned about their impact that their individual needs and self-expression are relegated to the dark corners of the mind. Neither is fulfilling, effective, nor the full possibility of who we can be as human beings.

We tend to get out of balance in different ways depending on our own unique personalities and contexts. We all have our defaults: In the word Co-Active, we have the very relational people who tend toward the Co, and the Active ones who are more focused on results. Some of us worry so much about making sure everyone is happy that nothing gets done; while others get captured by their to-do lists and sacrifice relationships in the process. Either side can run amok, and then we find ourselves swinging between polarities, reacting rather than creating. We think, "Oh dear, I got so focused on relationships I forgot about results, so everyone, march!" or "Oops, I forgot my family while I was working to get ahead, so here I am now, let's all connect—wait, where are you going?" It's a bit like a seesaw, one side bumping down to the ground, only to be shifted up to the sky by the other.

The challenge is learning to stand more and more in the hyphen. If you've ever tried balancing in the middle of a seesaw, you know it's not an inherently stable place to be, but requires continuous adjustments and recalibration. Holding the Co and the Active is dynamic, challenging, and ultimately, very effective.

It's also a bit of a paradox, which is part of what makes it so challenging. But as our world expands and becomes more complex it is essential that we learn to dance with paradox and hold two seemingly opposing ideas at the same time. While linear thinking was workable in a time when our world was simpler, we won't be able to navigate the challenges that face us unless we are able to be more expansive in our thinking and in our lives. We must learn to hold complexity and paradoxical ideas in order to resolve the challenges that face us. We need to learn to embrace the "yes, and" of life rather than the "either/or."

As we've said, the Co side of Co-Active corresponds both to the brain's right hemisphere and the default mode network. While it's not fair to our Active side (the left hemisphere and the task positive network) to say that Co is in charge of creativity, Co is the side that is comfortable with ambiguity, mystery, and what is unknown—and much can be created from there. However, when the seesaw is too far balanced to the Co side of things, relationships and dreaming may take precedence over action, over-empathizing and exploring possibilities. It can stop us from telling the truth and sometimes doing what really needs to be done, and things can become very bogged down as groups vision endlessly or look for absolute consensus so that no one is left out.

Jean is a successful executive in a Fortune 500 company. She was an effective leader and her team had a reputation for innovation and excellence in their projects. There was a true culture of camaraderie and her direct reports enjoyed working for her. She decided to hire a coach, however, because her annual performance reviews provided consistent feedback that she was being too much of a "Mother hen" with her team. The feedback from her boss was simple: Jean needed to "toughen up." And in her first coaching session, she herself said, "I have to learn to get tough. I keep being told I am too much of a caretaker. It's time to stop!"

The temptation would have been to bump the seesaw down to the opposite side by "getting tough," as her boss wanted her to do. But this would have meant being false to her own character and confusing and upsetting her team, who honestly loved, admired, and felt close to her. Instead, in the process of coaching she learned how to stand more and more in the middle, not leaving behind her loving nature and genuine care and empathy for her team, but bringing in more accountability and willingness to have difficult conversations when needed, ultimately becoming a powerful blend of rigor and kindness.

By being able to embrace the Active without losing the Co, she became the kind of leader she always wanted to be. She is now an inspiration to others in her organization who recognize her "magic touch." Her supervisors no longer tell her to "get tough." Instead, they bring her in when delicate negotiations need to be conducted because they know she will connect with people *and* hold the bottom line!

While Jean is a wonderful example of someone who needed to learn she could hold the paradox of integrating action and accountability with her deeply relational side, there are others whose lesson is the opposite. In these opposing cases, the Active side dominates. What becomes most important are results, actions, and accountability. The Active side is more concerned with individual trees than the whole forest and thus is excellent at details and particulars; it loves to see projects move forward in a linear and predictable manner.

When this side is over-calibrated, people's feelings may not be taken into account, not to mention vision and meaning. In the

Arbinger Institute's wonderful book, *The Anatomy of Peace*, there is a powerful description of how we view people when we are overly focused on the Active side of the seesaw: as either obstacles in our way, vehicles that can help us with our own agenda, or as simply irrelevant.

An example of a person living dominantly on the Active side is Peter, a career CFO who was promoted to a role of much greater leadership in a company that had a more "Co" than "Active" culture. A smart and accomplished man, he tended to be very linear and results-oriented. Because he understood he was in a relational culture, he was aware of the importance of relationships, but tried to "do" connection as if it were something on his list of tasks. He decided to work with a coach when he realized the checklist approach, while fine with numbers and to-do lists, wasn't effective with people.

Through coaching, he developed an understanding that relationship wasn't a thing he could do, but something that required a connection to his authentic heart, love for people, openness and vulnerability, and a willingness to not know the answer sometimes. Peter learned to stop, breathe, and get present with himself and the other person before jumping into the task at hand. The organization saw the changes and as a result people became much more willing to listen to and adopt more of his very valuable "Active" ideas and initiatives.

Being Co-Active offers a perspective that elevates us from the constraining mindset of the "good-bad" polarity. It's not that Jean was "too soft" and Peter "too tough;" it was that each needed to bring more in from the other side of the hyphen, and ultimately learn to stand more solidly in the center. Instead of blaming people for their limitations, we can say "yes, *and*." Yes, you are warm and approachable—don't lose that. *And* there is territory to explore on the side of being firm, clear, and discerning. And yes, you are realistic and focused—don't lose that. *And* there is something to be learned about getting people on board and feeling a part of things. Standing comfortably in the balance of the hyphen takes practice and patience, because we are expanding past well-established defaults, but over and over we have seen that this is the ultimate key to effectiveness in life and work.

Once again, we each have a default, a comfort zone that pulls us, especially when we are under stress. Those of us who are more "Co" may feel paralyzed, worrying that any forward motion runs the risk of hurting someone's feelings or that we may not have explored *every* possibility. Those of us who are more "Active" may feel driven to push no matter what. It's important to recognize our own tendencies and be on the lookout for default behaviors. It can be helpful to remember that we are at risk of bumping the seesaw all the way down on one side, and that the answer lies in standing in the center, in the hyphen.

Our friend James, a vice president in a large international company as well as a Co-Active coach, recently had this reflection about organizations: "The standard hierarchy addresses the complexity of a business by breaking things down into manageable pieces. We call these 'departments.' This is fine, but what comes with this approach is what we call 'silos,' where no one takes responsibility across the boundaries of the departments. Being Co-Active provides an answer for that in the hyphen, which represents the white space, the interface, and this is where leadership—co-leading—is desperately needed.

"In most organizations this goes unaddressed because there has been no model for how to lead there. I think it's why we see companies reorganize so often—they think the answer lies in how things are divided up. But of course with each reorganization, there are just new white spaces.

"When an organization is integrated, it is an amazing place to work. People are able to utilize infrastructure without being dominated by it. Responsibility is shared throughout the organization rather than being limited to a select few. Creativity increases dramatically as people are able to navigate uniquely in response to specific challenges, leaning into the efficiency and stability of an organizational structure without having the *structure* dominate what is possible."

In Conclusion

People desire to separate their worlds into polarities of dark and light, ugly and beautiful, good and evil, right and wrong, inside and outside. Polarities serve us in our learning and growth, but as souls we are all.
~Joy Page

Being Co-Active is emerging at a time when we have developed a greater capacity for complexity. Perhaps this is because modern society has driven us to it with the tremendous pace of change we find ourselves in at the beginning of the twenty-first century, or maybe our brains have developed a little more integrative structure than we have had in the past. Regardless, more and more we see people able to embrace paradox, to understand the limitations of polarity thinking, and to integrate themselves.

Standing in the hyphen is a healthy way of dealing with the strains and stresses of life as we know it today, because it gives us the ability to navigate complexity. And since life certainly isn't getting any simpler, this is a capacity we all desperately need. The great gift of over twenty years' exploration into being Co-Active all over the world (as of the writing of this book CTI has offered courses in twenty-five countries and eight languages; the book *Co-Active Coaching* has been translated into twelve languages) is that it has allowed us to see real, tangible human transformation again and again, by embracing the hyphen.

In organizations, we've seen people shift from a view that the bottom line is everything to an understanding that an organi-zation is a community made up of people with human concerns and emotions, *and* the bottom line is important. In relationships we've seen people understand that it's not my needs or your needs, it's *our* needs. And the list goes on. Again and again, clients, students, and others who have been touched by the philosophy and tools of being Co-Active tell us about the difference it has made in their lives—not just through coaching, but by embracing the philosophy and strategies of this methodology in day-to-day life.

In the following chapters we'll explore the philosophy and practical aspects of the Co-Active way, which provide a clear and accessible road map to standing in the hyphen and leading a more integrated life, from uniting silos to parenting more effectively, and everything in between.

Chapter Five

The Philosophy of Being Co-Active:
The Four Cornerstones

He who loves practice without theory is like the sailor who boards ship without a rudder and compass and never knows where he may cast.
~Leonardo da Vinci

The Co-Active model rests on four key cornerstones, which provide a philosophical underpinning and a guiding theory for what it is to be Co-Active. Although originally developed to help explain and guide the Co-Active coaching relationship, these cornerstones also apply and can be used in every area of life. Individually, each provides a powerful frame for relating to others and ourselves, for helping with either differentiation, linkage, or both. Taken together, they are much more than a coaching philosophy. The cornerstones are both container and map for a masterfully integrated life.

The magic of the cornerstones is that they are rooted in a stand for our fundamental interconnectedness. While many may see this as a spiritual view, it is also one that is profoundly pragmatic and practical. In other words, it's not necessary to see the Co-Active cornerstones through a spiritual lens in order to access their power. These are universal guideposts that provide the foundation for an effective life.

Chapter Three explored the concept of integration (the linkage of differentiated elements). In this chapter we'll begin to look at what it takes to live an integrated life by examining the distinctions and importance of each of the four key cornerstones of being Co-Active:

1. People Are Naturally Creative, Resourceful, and Whole
2. Dance in This Moment
3. Focus on the Whole Person
4. Evoke Transformation

We'll explore not only these cornerstones in depth, but also how each helps us connect more deeply with ourselves and one another, providing helpful direction for living a more integrated life.

Cornerstone #1: People Are Naturally Creative, Resourceful, and Whole

I am larger and better than I thought. I did not know I held so much goodness.
~Walt Whitman

The first and most important of the four cornerstones is the fundamental belief that people are naturally creative, resourceful, and whole. (This view certainly isn't CTI's alone, in fact, its roots trace back to psychologist Carl Rogers' view of human development, and is echoed in many psychological and coaching disciplines.) Because this is the most foundational of the cornerstones, we will spend more time exploring what it means.

We believe all people are naturally creative, resourceful, and whole. This cornerstone, however, involves far more than simply seeing the best in each other and ourselves. It is a fundamental view that people are inherently undamaged, capable, and inventive. They don't need to earn or learn this status; it is innate.

Breaking this cornerstone down to its components, we begin with *naturally*. By this we mean that people are born whole and complete. Imagine a newborn baby. No matter what the circumstances, they are born as a full expression of life and have inherent value. This is not something we learn. Being naturally creative, resourceful, and whole is a state of our essence and a gift of our birth and humanity.

After *naturally*, we have *creative*. By this we mean that people are able to evolve, change, and grow. We are "response-able," that is, able to respond to our surroundings rather than simply react; acting from choice rather than conditioning. We have a highly evolved prefrontal cortex, which means we are not limited by the reactivity of our mammalian and reptilian brains, which seek survival above all things. As humans, we can dream, imagine and create.

Next there is *resourceful*, meaning we are able to generate solutions to the challenges we face. We have within us what we need to be effective and to grow; we are "sufficient unto the day."

And finally, *whole*. This is a primary choice of one's personal perspective or worldview. Do we choose to see life as whole or as broken? Choosing wholeness helps to create order in a random universe. If our view is wholeness, we can see that things fit together on some level. As studies in chaos theory have shown, patterns emerge from seemingly random events when one steps back far enough and has enough data. Holding this cornerstone means that even if we can't see wholeness, we trust it's there.

This is a profoundly respectful and empowering way to view human beings, and key to integration because we are differentiating (others and ourselves) as whole, complete, undamaged, and unbroken. And, as we saw in Chapter Three, differentiation supports and allows space for powerful linkage. When we see ourselves as naturally creative, resourceful, and whole, we can link with another from a place of completeness and strength—not from a codependent place because we are hoping the other will fix or save us, and not from an overly independent place because we are afraid they will intrude. And, of course, the same is true when we hold another as naturally creative, resourceful, and whole. We can allow them to link with us from their innate wholeness, dancing with what you have to offer and celebrating what is different while remaining connected.

It's important to note that this cornerstone calls for a clear distinction between fundamental essence and behavior. It's true that people do awful things and have awful things done to them. We can become separated from our naturally creative, resourceful, and whole self. And yet this is like the sun going behind the clouds; we know it is still there even though it's obscured from our view. In most of life, we have been taught to interact with people's behavior, judging and evaluating them based on what they do, rather than looking for their essence underneath it all. Holding the cornerstone of naturally creative, resourceful, and whole calls us to engage with people at the level of their essence while having appropriate boundaries for their behavior when needed.

A powerful example of this comes from CTI's work in a federal prison in Littleton, Colorado. In 2004, twenty-six male inmates participated in Co-Active coach training. From the beginning they were taught about—and held as—naturally creative, resourceful, and whole. When the cornerstone was introduced in the first class, they rolled their eyes. They *knew* they were broken. After all, the majority had been viewed as problematic their whole lives—starting early on with being "naughty" then moving on to being juvenile delinquents and finally becoming defined as criminals.

However, in the CTI classes the leaders pushed them to discover what they could do, and didn't back off or take care of them when they blustered, resisted, or shut down. When one leader was moved to tears, a big guy in the back of the room said gruffly, "You can cry all you want, I will not be doing *any* crying." But later, during an acknowledgment exercise, he and others found they had tears in their eyes, deeply moved by the process. For most, it was the first time they had ever been seen as human beings separate from their behavior.

The leaders insisted that they find the naturally creative, resourceful, and whole human being in each other. And, as one leader later reported, "they turned to this like sunflowers turn to the sun." By the end of five three-day workshops on coaching, profound changes occurred in the ways the inmates saw each other and themselves. Possibilities other than fighting and dominance emerged and a culture of peer coaching and conflict resolution, rather than escalation, began to be part of the norm.

Even apart from the extreme example of prison inmates, it's true that in most cultures we are not socialized to view each other or ourselves as naturally creative, resourceful, and whole. We are generally taught that people are flawed, sinful, and damaged, in need of fixing or changing. We are trained to spot the problem and solve it. At best, this leads to a desire to be overly helpful, taking on other people's problems as our own; at worst, it can lead to exclusion and damaging judgment, leaving people feeling they can never measure up or be good enough to fit in.

Holding people naturally creative, resourceful, and whole is a radical act, one that liberates both them and ourselves. Stephanie is a single mom who adopted two boys on her own. These brothers came to her from the foster care system when they were six and sixteen. The older brother was failing in high school and carrying the impact of fetal alcohol syndrome. By the time he was eighteen, she had fairly low expectations for him: "I just want him to stay out of jail and get some sort of job," she shared. That year, while he did graduate, he and his girlfriend also became pregnant. And so Stephanie, not quite forty, became a grandmother. Stephanie had taken some classes in Co-Active principles and was doing her best to live them in her day-to-day life. She was able to sit calmly with her son and his girlfriend, helping them explore their options and make plans that worked for them. While the rest of the family got lost in judgment and drama, Stephanie found that she was able to stay present and focused on what mattered: helping her son and his girlfriend figure out how to be young parents to the best of their ability.

Reflecting on her son and the situation, she says, "The only thing that has gotten me through this is remembering that Darton is naturally creative, resourceful, and whole. My job is to love him, support him, and provide resources if he wants them. It's not my job to live his life." By lessening the overall drama and keeping close ties between all the parties involved, more than two years later she has been able to contribute to a caring and stable environment for the young child, who is now a toddler doing great, surrounded by a loving family on all sides.

Andrea also found that holding people naturally creative, resourceful, and whole was powerful in her work relationships. "I'm a nice Midwestern girl at heart," she shared. "I am well-trained to be self-deprecating and not to cause any trouble. When I learned about people being naturally creative, resourceful, and whole, I started realizing how often I turned down offers of help. For example, instead of gratefully accepting when one of my colleagues says they can help out during a time I am really pressed, I always say, 'Oh, thanks, I can do it,' because I know they are busy too. One day I had a real *aha* moment, and I saw that maybe people wouldn't offer if they didn't want to! So now, instead of the battle where I make *sure* I am not causing a problem before I accept any help, I just tell myself to say thank you and trust that if they didn't actually want to help me, they wouldn't offer. And you know what? Life is smoother, easier, and my colleagues and I are a better team now that I can gracefully accept their support. It's like my being willing to say, 'Yes, you can help,' has changed the way we interact, so I am leaning more on them and they are also leaning more on me."

As Andrea realized, it's all too common that we don't ask for help or tell each other the truth because we feel we are somehow protecting them. But when we do this, we stay separate from each other rather than build the authentic trust all effective relationships require.

Andrea offers a simple but powerful example of how we can differentiate and link by holding others naturally creative, resourceful, and whole. She was able to *differentiate* by honoring that they are being authentic when they offer to help, and then *link* by accepting that help. By worrying about being a burden, she was actually creating separateness. By trusting that others can make their own decisions, for which she is not responsible, she can link.

In being Co-Active, we do not see people as broken or deficient, and this is critical to how our brains engage with other people's brains. First of all, when we hold ourselves and others as naturally creative, resourceful, and whole, we level the playing field. We don't position ourselves as higher or lower, smarter or stupider, more or less developed. This is important because the brain is highly reactive to perceived threats to status. Research by emotional intelligence expert Richard Boyatzis and colleagues found that when participants in a study were evaluated by others and therefore risked a reduction in status, their cortisol levels (an indicator of stress) remained higher for 50 percent longer. And when the brain is influenced by the chemicals associated with stress, it is less creative and less able to think of long-term solutions.

When we stand in the cornerstone of holding others naturally creative, resourceful, and whole there is no judgment or evaluation in any given relationship—whether it is with another or with ourselves. This allows people to remain open to input and more able to access their own unique creativity. Holding people naturally creative, resourceful, and whole means we ask rather than tell, are curious rather than judgmental, and assume that ultimately everyone can find their own solutions and make their own choices.

It's also interesting to note there is substantial evidence that expectations shape experience. If we truly see someone as whole, we will look for (and find) evidence of this wholeness. Just as we begin to notice red Toyotas everywhere after we've purchased one, what we are "primed" to see influences what we notice, remember, and put our attention on.

There is a classic example of this in an experiment from the sixties by a professor from Harvard University. Teachers in an elementary school were told some students were "late bloomers" and that they were about to have a dramatic improvement in their academic abilities. In reality, the kids were randomly selected and were no more special or different than their class-mates. But at the end of the year they had not only performed better in the eyes of their teachers, they also scored significantly higher on standardized IQ tests. In other words, what the teachers expected had a significant impact on how the students performed.

In business, this same phenomenon is sometimes called the Pygmalion effect because of the 1988 *Harvard Business Review* article, "Pygmalion in Management," by J. Sterling Livingston. In this groundbreaking essay, which looks at the evidence for the ways in which expectations shape performance, Sterling says quite directly, "The way managers treat their subordinates is subtly influenced by what they expect of them."

Holding people naturally creative, resourceful, and whole also means we don't have to take on their problems. This is one of the things coaches most often encourage people to embrace as they fret and worry about what to do about this person or that person, what will happen if they do or don't say this or that, and so on. We'll ask them, "What if your mother, son, friend, or employee were naturally creative, resourceful, and whole? What if it wasn't your job to fix anything?" And while this is often an unusual idea for some people to get their heads around, we start seeing stress and worry decrease as they are able to embrace it. More than just a philosophy of coaching, holding people as naturally creative, resourceful and whole is a powerful way of engaging with day-to-day life.

Tips and Tools overview

In each section, we will provide a set of tips and tools for you to use to bring this cornerstone more fully to your life. Because everyone learns and integrates differently, we've given you some options ranging from things to ponder to structured activities. The tips and tools sections are divided as follows:

1) *A Few Things to Think About.* The title says it all—simply some things to think about. There is nothing in particular you need to do (although you might find yourself discussing or even journaling about the topic if you feel like it). You may also find that a shift in thinking inspires new actions.

2) *A Few Simple Things to Do in your Day-to-Day Life.* These are things you can do without a lot of extra effort as you go through your day-to-day life—easy ways to integrate the cornerstone into your daily activities.

3) *Exercises for Developing this Cornerstone.* These are more focused ways you can intentionally build the muscle of the cornerstone. In this section, we provide structured activities and instructions. We hope you'll find time to try a few!

Tips and Tools for Cornerstone One: Holding people as naturally creative, resourceful and whole

1) A Few Things to Think About

- Naturally creative, resourceful, and whole is about letting go of our judgments and opinions, desire to control, and our need to fix everything. What would happen if you took your hands off the steering wheel and let go? What might open up?

- When people are facing a big challenge, it's more powerful, useful, and motivating when they find their own solutions. When we believe in someone else, it is about *them*, and it can take courage on your part to trust that they will be OK.

How can you find the courage to let those you care about find their own way?

- We all have indicators/cues for when we have slipped into not holding people as naturally creative, resourceful and whole, and it's helpful to know what our own are. Think about whether you do any of the following:
  - Become overly careful, be "nice" instead of real
  - Get irritated and or frustrated by what you perceive as "bad" choices or decisions by others
  - Check out emotionally

2) A Few Simple Things to Do in your Day-to-Day Life
- When you feel worried or overwhelmed by the problems of the people around you, take a moment to visualize these burdens like a bag you are setting down gently on the ground. Notice the relief of this new lightness and freedom.
- Open-ended questions are a powerful tool for engaging creativity in others. When you are about to give advice, here are a few questions you can try instead:
  - What's most important to you?
  - What's challenging about this situation?
  - What ideas do you have to move forward?
  - What would you like from me?
- Acknowledgement can help people take a larger view of themselves. Make a habit of telling people things like:
  - I believe in you.
  - I know you will be able to figure this out.
  - You have everything you need to resolve this successfully.

Note: We can only hold others naturally creative, resourceful and whole to the degree that we see ourselves this way, so you might also try this on yourself!

3) Exercises for Developing this Cornerstone
- Pick a relationship in your life where you are frustrated or feel burdened. How might you be failing to hold this person as naturally creative, resourceful and whole? What might you say or ask for if you did? Make a list of three new actions that you will take in this relationship based on holding the other person naturally creative, resourceful and whole. What shifts between you?
- Find a "naturally creative, resourceful and whole" buddy to help you stay connected to this cornerstone. One organization we know of that embraced being Co-Active actually started a monthly "naturally creative, resourceful and whole" lunch club, where they talked about the challenges and progress they were having with peers, employees, partners and families.

Cornerstone #2: Dance in This Moment

Why not just live in the moment, especially if it has a good beat?
~Goldie Hawn

The second cornerstone is the commitment to *dance in this moment*. Being Co-Active stands on the dedication to being fully present in the here and now, open and flexible and ready to respond. Dancing in this moment means letting go of the past, which we cannot change, and also resisting the urge to send our energy to the future in the shape of needless worry and fear. As Mark Twain so wisely said, "My life has been filled with terrible misfortunes, most of which never happened."

Dancing in this moment truly requires standing on the hyphen between "Co" and "Active." We need to be aware of what is emerging and how we are feeling, moving toward inspired action from that point. When we dance in this moment with another person, we honor the energy of what is right here, right now. This is the only way to connect on the deepest level, because we are not dancing with who they once were in the past, or should be in the future, but rather with who they actually *are*, right now.

Thus, it's clear that this cornerstone is a key aspect of linkage, but it is also important to differentiation. To dance in this moment means seeing and knowing someone (or ourselves) as what is present *now*. When we see others or ourselves as someone in the past or future, we create a phantom or a mask with whom to link, not a true, complex, and emergent human being.

To dance in this moment means life develops without a program or script. Instead, we're called to follow the movement of what is occurring in each moment, staying connected and flowing with the ups and downs of any situation.

Dancing in this moment means looking for an opportunity to create rather than being constrained by circumstances. Jeff was the founder and CEO of a medium-sized business in the service industry. The economic downturn of 2008 found his company hit hard, and he faced losing it all. His CFO advised laying off 25 percent of the workforce in order to stay afloat. Jeff reluctantly wrote a speech announcing the layoffs, dreading having to give his loyal workforce such terrible news, but trusting his CFO that it was the only way. But when he got up to the podium to give the speech, he found he couldn't. He looked out at the people who had helped build his company, and threw his carefully prepared talk away. "I knew it was the 'right' thing to do, the practical thing," he reported. "But it just didn't sit well with me. There were no other jobs in our industry at the time—what were those people going to do? I literally felt sick to my stomach when I thought of letting a quarter of them go. And I was afraid that if we did the layoffs we'd lose forever the positive, effective culture we'd created over the years." So instead of giving the prepared speech, he sat on the edge of the stage, looked out at the expectant crowd, and asked himself, what's needed here, right now?

Jeff connected with the crowd and openly told them the truth of the situation. "I told them where we were and what we needed in order to survive. And I listened to them. I didn't have a clue what I was going to do, but as we talked the idea came to me that maybe we could do pay cuts for everyone, and achieve the same results." Jeff stepped into the moment and opened his heart, and in relationship with his workforce, found a new way. The staff embraced the pay cuts, and the company made it through the downturn. "Now that the economy has improved, our business is stronger than ever," Jeff said. "I wouldn't have thought of that solution on my own—I would have assumed no one would go along with it. But together, well, something became possible I couldn't have done alone."

Jeff danced in this moment in an incredibly difficult situation. Instead of reacting from fear, he was present in the moment and looked at the reality of the circumstances in terms of what was possible. When we are open to possibilities, we are far more effective. We can't dance with problems—they make us want to move away, create distance from what is uncomfortable. This makes us victims of the circumstances of our lives. Dancing in this moment means patiently embracing and holding circumstances as possibilities, while being open to where things might go.

There is classic Chinese teaching story about a man and horse we think beautifully illustrates the power—and challenge—of dancing in this moment. A farmer has a beautiful horse, the envy of all his neighbors. One night, it runs away. The neighbors say, "Oh, that is terrible, you lost your horse!" And the man says, "Who knows what is good and what is bad? We'll see."

A week later, the horse comes back, and he has with him a lovely coal-black mare. The neighbors say, "Oh, you are so lucky! What good fortune to have two horses instead of one!" And the man says, "Who knows what is good and what is bad? We'll see."

The man's son loves to ride the mare, who is wild and fiery. One day, they are galloping across a field, and the horse shies away from a snake. The son is thrown off and breaks his leg quite badly. The neighbors say, "Oh that is terrible! You must rue the day that horse came to your farm!" And the man says, "Who knows what is good and what is bad? We'll see."

Shortly thereafter, the army comes through town, conscripting all the young men for a terrible bloody war that is waging in the east. The man's son is spared due to his disability. The neighbors again cry, "Oh, you are so lucky!" And the man says, "Who knows what is good and what is bad? We'll see."

Dancing in this moment requires this sort of "we'll see" attitude. It also calls us to stay aware of the *why* of what we are doing, something many of us don't question nearly enough.

A study was once done with a group of monkeys. They put them in a cage with a bunch of bananas out of reach and a ladder underneath the bananas. Of course, one of the monkeys immediately went to climb the ladder to get the bananas, but as he did, the experimenter sprayed him with cold water, while also spraying those sitting on the floor. Another monkey tried, and she was sprayed as well, as were all the others. Very quickly the monkeys learned that climbing the ladder meant being cold, wet and miserable, so they simply stopped trying to get the bananas.

After a while, the researchers replaced one of the monkeys with a new monkey, who, spotting the bananas, went to climb the ladder. The other monkeys pulled her off right away. When another new monkey was brought in and attempted to reach the bananas, all the monkeys pulled him off, including the one who had never been sprayed.

This went on, with the researchers switching out old monkeys for new. Each new monkey quickly joined in the behavior, even though there was no longer any punishment. After a while, the original monkey group was entirely gone, and all there were left were monkeys who had never experienced the cold water. And still, they pulled each new monkey off the ladder as they attempted to reach the bananas.

This metaphor of monkeys shunning the ladder shows up in our day-to-day lives. Karen recently saw she was doing it in certain areas herself. "I was doing it in the way I manage people at work, for example, our performance reviews. We've always followed standard procedures, but honestly I hate them, and it never occurred to me to question whether there is another way. I was just going along with the way you're 'supposed' to do it, without ever questioning whether it is truly effective."

As Karen realized, once you stop and ask why, the context expands and there is more meaning in everything you are doing. How many of us do things the way we always have, or the way someone else does, without questioning whether it actually makes sense? To dance in this moment means staying present in the *now*, embracing curiosity rather than simply accepting "that's the way it is."

Dancing in this moment is also about presence and attention, and there is evidence that our presence has a profound effect on others. According to research by the Institute of HeartMath, "a subtle yet influential electromagnetic or 'energetic' communication system operates just below our conscious awareness... (and this) field plays an important role in communicating physiological, psychological, and social information between individuals." HeartMath has found that these fields impact each other. Over time, a more organized and stable field will positively impact a less "coherent" one. In other words, just as metronomes set ticking at different beats will align themselves to the same tempo, our hearts naturally synch with each other.

When we dance in this moment—being present, flexible, and open—we bring a greater sense of coherence to the energetic field that surrounds us. This impacts those around us in positive ways that are not in conscious awareness, bringing a sense of calm and presence. When we dance in this moment, it's common for people to say things to us like, "I always feel so much better just talking to you."

Gregory is a supervising emergency room doctor who is working to create a Co-Active culture on his team. One of the tricks he has created for dancing in this moment is what he calls "Purell moments." "I saw that one thing we do all the time in a hospital setting is to use the Purell sanitizers," he said. "During stressful times, I started to simply be present in the moment each time I used one. Just focusing on what I was doing—even for an instant—immediately made me a little calmer and able to carry on in a more effective way. I realized it was particularly helpful when I was dealing with a difficult person. I could maintain my center and we got through things much more easily."

Gregory taught the nurses and aides this simple technique, and it began to be a habit with almost everyone. "You'd see a nurse come out of a patient room, use the Purell, and take a deep breath. One day I was in a meeting with other areas of the hospital and the OR people said to me, 'Hey, what's going on down in Emergency, anyway? You guys are so much easier to deal with these days.' I know this simple trick of being more present in the moment has made a huge difference for everyone."

Research in the field of mindfulness also points towards many more benefits of being present, focused and attentive. For example, according to a recent *Scientific American* article, a 2012 study found that presence may actually be linked to longer life. People who have a greater propensity toward mind wandering were found to have shorter telomeres at the end of their chromosomes than those who tended to stay more in the present. And shorter telomeres are associated with shorter cell life. In essence, dancing in this moment may not just be more effective, it may literally lengthen our lifespan!

In addition, according to brain expert Daniel Siegel, the process of having "collaborative, contingent conversations" that are emotionally attuned and non-directive builds positive neural connections in the brain. These conversations are similar to the best relationships of early development, when a primary caregiver is responsive and open to the needs of a child. There is a give and take in this dance of affection and love, which creates an ideal container for learning and growth. While being Co-Active with each other is by no means an attempt to re-parent, according to research, connected conversation with someone who is present and open cannot help but have a positive impact on the brain.

Tips and Tools for Cornerstone Two: Dance in This Moment

1) A Few Things to Think About
- When a problem comes up (and of course they will!), try looking for the opportunity or even the blessing it holds. A shift in thinking like this is a proven stress-reliever and can open up powerful creativity.
- Think about your own "monkey on the ladder" beliefs and behaviors. Instead of just going along with "the way it's always been done," ask yourself why—for the sake of what? This will allow you to be more present to what's needed now.

2) A Few Simple Things to Do in your Day-to-Day Life
- If you don't already have one, create a habit of being more present. It's okay to start small. One person we know wrote a large "P" in nail polish on her shampoo bottle, which reminded her to simply be-here-now in the shower every day. She reported that she was then able to expand this into being more present in every moment, especially when circumstances were more challenging.
- Sometimes we have habits that take us out of engaging with the present moment. For example, those of us who tend to think out loud may jump in prematurely without paying close attention to what is being said. Try going into

your next meeting practicing listening longer before responding. Those of us who process internally, on the other hand, may tend to wait until the moment is past. Try going into your next meeting with a commitment to blurting more quickly. See what happens.

3) Exercises for Developing this Cornerstone
- Here is a simple practice for being more present that you can do at any time, whether you're driving in the car or sitting in a meeting. Just focus for a moment on each of these three things:
  ○ Find your feet
  ○ Find your seat
  ○ Find your breath
- Pick a relationship where you tend to get triggered into old patterns or behaviors. Here are some helpful questions to journal about:
  ○ What is the story I tell myself about this relationship and why it is hard/difficult etc?
  ○ What is the evidence that I have collected to support my story (examples of behaviors the other person has said or done)?
  ○ What might be possible if I set this story aside?
- Next time you are with this person, practice "find your feet, find your seat, find your breath" and journal about what happens in your relationship.

Cornerstone #3: Focus on the Whole Person

I realized that I had screwed up my life living different parts of my life in different places. I wasn't whole. I wasn't integrated. I wasn't a complete person.
~James McGreevey (former Governor of New Jersey)

The third cornerstone is *focus on the whole person*. When we relate to the entire heart, mind, body, and spirit of those around us, rather than focusing on individual aspects, we then see them as more than the sum of their parts, the role they play, or labels they've been assigned (CFO, dad, dyslexic). We can understand and respect them as the entire, complex beings that they are. And for ourselves, focus on the whole person means tapping into the wealth of data and information available to us from our whole being, not just our rational brain.

We often tend to interact with each other in a "role-to-role" way: boss to employee, parent to child, doctor to patient, etc. But inside every role-to-role relationship, there are two complex, layered, and even contradictory human beings. (Again we are reminded of the Walt Whitman quote, "Do I contradict myself? Very well then, I contradict myself. I am large, I contain multitudes.") And so, we tend to try to fit our multitudes into these narrow roles as required, which not only is ultimately soul-numbing and frustrating, it limits creativity, innovation, and effectiveness.

Roles are essential for a healthy infrastructure—it's important to know who does what—but when we are *only* roles the complexity gets lost. Focus on the whole person calls us to extend our understanding well beyond the convenience of simple labels and roles and see ourselves and each other as the complexity we are—a complexity that includes whatever role we may be filling in the moment.

It's an uncomfortable truth that we tend to want people to be like us, so we often try to get rid of behaviors and ideas that are counter to our own. In doing this, we lose in creativity what we gain in so-called efficiency, and risk, as the monkeys earlier illustrated for us, doing things that don't work over and over again without questioning. In conformity we become less efficient. The power is, again, in the *linkage* of *differentiated* parts. Focus on the whole person is about understanding that each person's wholeness is their own differentiation, and this is the gift they bring to the enterprise.

For ourselves, focus on the whole person is a reminder to listen to the many voices within. Our rational mind has wisdom, but so do our body and spirit, and they are valuable allies and resources as well. Jane is an interesting example of this. A long-time independent consultant, she recently took a job working for a company three days a week. While the tasks were similar to those she performed as a consultant, the experience of working in a windowless office with colleagues who were often frustrated and negative quickly began taking its toll.

She reflected, "My brain keeps telling me this is fine, look at the good money you are making, look at the interesting work in front of you. But my body is miserable. I have a cough, I seem to keep injuring myself, and I am tired all the time." After only three months of trying her hardest to be "rational" about the job, she finally decided her body might be wiser in this area than her brain. "I can tell myself I am happy, but my body knows I'm not. It's time to listen."

Neuroscience teaches us that we are amazingly complex and multilayered beings—and the more we can integrate and be agile with this complexity, the better. While in the past, the argument may have been for developing one aspect over another (for example, the heavy emphasis on rationality and logic over emotion and intuition in business), there is evidence from current research that the most emotionally intelligent and effective people are those who can use the gifts of different parts of their brain together effectively.

For example, research by Richard Boyatzis and others at Case Western Reserve University used functional Magnetic Resonance Imaging (fMRI, aka "brain scans") to look at the brain states of both leaders and their teams. They found that leaders who created the most emotionally open and "resonant" state in their followers had more brain integration themselves. That is, more areas of their brain fired—including both the right and left hemisphere—in coordinated ways than in the brains of less effective leaders.

This cornerstone points to integration within the self— honoring and harmonizing every aspect of our being. Those of us who tend toward the relational side also need to be able to move things forward in an "active" manner. And even the most driven among us need their "co" aspects that point toward relationships, meaning, and presence.

As in all things, the more we integrate our own complex qualities and attributes, the more we can help others do so as well. As we saw in Chapter Three, integration releases us from polarity thinking, from holding things in the either/or paradigm that leads to separation. The cornerstone of *focus on the whole person* speaks to seeing each other—and also, as always, ourselves—as this *and* that, not this *or* that.

Focus on the whole person also means not dealing only with the presenting issue. It calls us instead to look further than fixing the problem, to also explore thoughts and feelings, and give voice to intuitive gut reactions. This kind of attention literally helps integrate different parts of the brain, which opens up new solutions and creativity, and also builds lasting connections that can be used for future problem-solving.[2]

Another aspect of this cornerstone is the ever-present challenge for many of us regarding work-life balance. As a manager or supervisor, the cornerstone of focus on the whole person means understanding people as more than cogs in the wheel of productivity, and honoring the fact that each of us has multiple roles that call for our attention. We are employees, bosses, daughters, sons, parents, piano players, artists, hikers, and cat-lovers. A Co-Active manager knows a balanced and fulfilled employee will be more engaged and ultimately more productive.

For example, Mandy works for a large international company. She is deeply dedicated to her job in human resources, which involves a great deal of training and one-on-one work with employees. The company has been working to create a Co-Active culture, and Mandy and her manager Eduardo have very much embraced this. "I really trust him," Mandy reported recently. "The other day, I told him that I love what I am doing, but the one-to-one work is exhausting. When I've had four employees in a row in for counseling, I am beat. He not only understood and empathized, he actually told me to take a nap if I needed to! He said he knows what an amazing job I am doing, and he wants me to be able to continue. If taking a nap keeps me from burning out, then that's what I should do. I feel like he sees me as so much more than just what I can do for him or the company, and you know, in today's corporate world, that's kind of rare."

Another example of this comes from Martin, who worked in a large nonprofit that was undergoing expansion. A new coworker was hired at his level, and from the start they butted heads. He felt she was overly critical in meetings, and didn't honor the context of where the organization had been. He began to regularly gossip and complain to another coworker, and the two of them quickly found they were creating an "us" and "them" club, where the new coworker was left out.

At one point, Martin realized he was spending a lot of energy on negativity toward this person. "When Rachel (the other coworker) and I would go to lunch, all we would talk about was what annoying thing Debbie had done that day," he said. "To be honest, it was sort of fun, but I'd come back to my desk ramped up and churning. One day I realized I'd made her into sort of a caricature. Plus, I was being a jerk. So Rachel and I made a deal to stop gossiping for three months, and to our credit, we honored it. For me, it wasn't even really about Debbie—I just didn't want to be such a negative person any more."

During the three months of not talking about Debbie, both Martin and Rachel noticed that somehow she became less annoying. One day, Martin and Debbie found themselves both leaving the building to take a walk over lunch, and without much thought, Martin invited her to walk with him. "I found out so much on that walk," he said. "This person I had spent my time complaining about was actually kind of funny. And she was really smart, which I had never given her credit for. But more important, I learned that she was just getting over a difficult custody battle and was caring for an aging parent, both of which had sapped her energy. She even said, with no prompting from me, that she felt she hadn't made a very good first impression! From that day forward, she was a completely different person to me, and when she was critical in meetings, I listened for the contribution she had instead of writing her off. She *always* had amazing ideas, and when I was connected instead of judging her, I saw that her perspective was usually just what we needed."

Lou even practiced focusing on the whole person with his daughter. He was cooking dinner, and Alberta, age four and a fussy eater, had agreed to try mushrooms with her spaghetti. She asked for them to be room temperature, and Lou's immediate response was to say no, just eat your dinner, we don't have time to let the mushrooms cool down. "Then I realized that when I cook for myself, I make things just the way I want them and never question my right to have preferences," he said. "But with my daughter, as much as I intend to let her find her own way, there are still times I find myself just wanting her to follow the plan. In this case, when I had that aha, I stopped myself from just saying no outright and told her that she had every right to ask for things the way she wanted them, but tonight we were in kind of a hurry so there wasn't time to let the mushrooms cool, so would it be okay to eat them warm? Instead of the usual resistance and battle, she just looked at me and said, 'Okay, Dad,' and ate them. I am seeing the value of always viewing her as a whole person, even though I know I have a certain role to play as her parent. And it is so much easier and more fun this way."

There is a story by spiritual teacher Anthony De Mello, from his book *Awakening: Conversations with the Master*. "One day the

Master was asked, 'What do you want your daughter to be when she grows up?' He replied without blinking an eye, 'Outrageously happy.'"

Tips and Tools for Cornerstone Three: Focus on the Whole Person

1) A Few Things to Think About

- It's normal to compare ourselves to others, and at times this can even be inspiring, but far too often comparison leaves us feeling that we personally are lacking. Begin to notice your automatic comparisons—whether positive (I am better than so and so) or negative (I am not as good as so and so). The act of comparing ourselves to others only serves to increase our sense of separation. In terms of focusing on the whole person, the truth is, we are all lacking in some areas and gifted in others.

- Ask yourself who you tend to think of as primarily their role, or one personality trait, or even as a sort of caricature. What would happen if you were curious about other aspects of their being?

2) A Few Simple Things to Do in your Day-to-Day Life

- Instead of telling yourself, "I should be more like so and so," practice saying, "While I am good at many things, I would like to expand my own capacity for _____" (whatever you admire in the other person).

- When someone is annoying you (for example, in a meeting), practice imagining all the competing roles they are playing. The more you actually know about them, the easier it is to do this.

- As simple as it may seem, one of the easiest ways to build the "muscle" of this cornerstone is to simply get to know people. If there is someone in your life with whom your relationship is strained or difficult, get to know them. Find out their story and discover who they are beneath the surface they present. One of our friends took on something she called "the go to lunch project." Whenever she felt a lack of connection, irritability or judgment with or about someone in her workplace, she took them to lunch and asked them about their lives. Each time, she felt the negative emotions ease and workflow improve.

3) Exercises for Developing this Cornerstone
- When you need or want to make a decision, try using this diagram as a way to bring in the many aspects of yourself.
- For an even deeper exploration, try this "House of You" visualization:

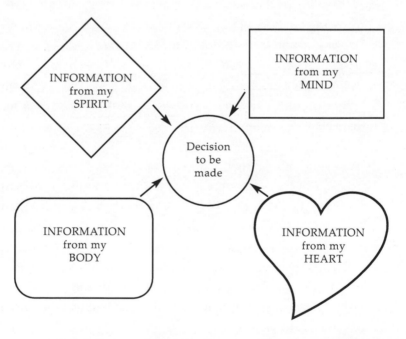

- Take three deep breaths and let each one go with a little sound. Let your breath move easily in and out, and let your body relax. Now imagine that you are someplace in nature—someplace that you really love. Perhaps it is the ocean, or a cool mountain forest or a meadow filled with wildflowers. Whatever place fills you with joy and happiness, go there now.

○ It is a beautiful day and the sun is shining brightly, kissing your skin wherever it touches. Ahead of you, you see a little path that looks completely inviting and you begin to walk along it.

○ There is the slightest breeze blowing and it ruffles your hair slightly and brushes across the back of your hands as you walk. All around you, you hear the sounds of nature. Perhaps it is the long roll of the ocean waves, or the rustle of the trees. Or maybe the lazy hum of insects in the shade. It smells so *good*—fresh and clean and delicious.

○ Just ahead, you see a little clearing with a house. This is the *House of You*. Take a moment to create the House of You in whatever way is most pleasing to you. Is this House of You small and cozy or stately and grand? In your mind's eye, create the House of You. (Pause)

○ The house is so inviting and enticing that it draws you closer, and as you approach, you see over the doorway a sign that says, "The House of..." and there's your name.

○ You easily and effortlessly move inside of this House of You. As you are standing inside, you notice that there are so many areas or rooms for you to explore. You could spend a lifetime exploring this House of You and never know it fully. Completely unique and totally inviting... The House of You.

○ Just off to the left, you notice an area or a room called "The Room of My Emotions." Oh, that sounds interesting... and you slip inside to explore. What do you find here? Is it light or dark? Is there furniture or not at all? Take a few moments to explore. (Pause)

○ You move out of this room now, knowing that you can

come back any time you wish... you know the way. Just off to your right you find another area or room... "The room of my Body" and you slip inside. What are the sights and sounds and sensations that await you here in the Room of your Body? Take a little time to explore. (Pause)

o And now you move out of the Room of your Body and just off to your left you see another room or area... "The Room of my Heart Mind"... that place of courage and action from the heart. So you slip into the Room of your Heart Mind. What do you sense and see and smell and feel? (Pause)

o Now you slip easily out of this room and off to your right you find another area... "The Room of My Spirit." And you move inside this room to discover and explore. What do you find in the Room of your Spirit? (Pause)

o Moving back into the central part of the House of You... you see so many, many rooms waiting to be explored and discovered... the unique complexity of you... there is no other on earth quite like you.

o One more room to explore before you go... "The Room of My..." and you choose the name. The Room of My _____ ... and you fill it in. (Pause)

o It's almost time to go... before you leave you might want to say a little blessing or a prayer of thanks to this incredible House of You. Or you might want to leave a little gift behind. Do whatever feels right to you now. (Pause)

o And so you turn to go, knowing that you can come back any time you wish to visit and explore this House of You. You slip outside into the waiting sunshine and began making your way along the path... walking.

o Returning now to the present moment, take a deep breath and wiggle your fingers or toes. You might want to stretch and move your body a little and when you feel ready, open your eyes.

Cornerstone #4: Evoke Transformation

We no longer need to fear arguments, confrontations or any kind of problems with ourselves or others. Even stars collide, and out of their crashing new worlds are born.
~Charlie Chaplin

More than simple change or the resolution of certain issues in life, the fourth cornerstone, *evoke transformation*, means that we are committed to fundamental shifts at the level of our essence or identity, not just shifts in the circumstances of our lives. When people experience these kinds of shifts, life flows far more effectively. And when we stand in this cornerstone, challenging circumstances become a forum for our development and growth. In fact, the more difficult the issue, the more we are called to become something greater than who we have been.

Being Co-Active calls us into the space of continuous learning, and of creating for ourselves and others lasting, positive change. All of us long for more effective ways of interacting with our jobs, families, and world. Ideally, we are interested in moving to the next level of human development as we continue to grow and expand our consciousness. We hope perhaps life can be more than simply managing a to-do list; we wonder if we can develop new capacities to navigate whatever life throws our way.

This cornerstone was (like the other cornerstones) created originally as a way of being for Co-Active coaches, an approach to help their clients with more than solutions to their problems. But (as with all the cornerstones) we believe this philosophy applies to all of us, whether we're coaches, parents, managers, teachers, or just human beings. A life where we are evoking transformation in ourselves and others is dynamic, powerful, impactful, and truly fulfilling.

At some deep level we know that we are here to contribute, and to develop. We sometimes forget that we don't have to accomplish some grand thing in order to make a real difference. Being with each other from the perspective of evoking transformation is fulfilling and powerful not because everything gets checked off the to-do list, but because we see human evolution before our very eyes.

Stefan was told he had an anger problem. His job as a stock trader exposed him to constant pressure and required he make lightning quick decisions constantly. His response to an overload of stress was to be continually sarcastic and often blow his top. After a painful calling on the carpet by his boss, he worked hard to shift this behavior, and to his credit, out of sheer force of will (and fear of losing his job), he did.

But after a year or so, he hired a coach because although he now felt he had his anger "under control" since he was no longer allowing himself the outbursts that once were common, he was still being passed over for advancement. Ironically, he found he was getting pulled back into his old patterns due to his frustration over not being recognized as having gotten "better." In coaching, Stefan saw that managing his anger wasn't just a question of keeping himself from blowing up while his real feelings simmered just below the surface. He realized that he needed to learn to ask positively for the opportunities he wanted, focus on being collaborative and helpful, and trust that he would eventually get the respect he so badly wanted.

His coach helped him realize that being angry over people not seeing that he had changed was simply evidence that he had, in fact, not actually changed. Upon understanding this, Stefan worked hard to make an authentic shift. He learned some new skills for being present to his anger without suppressing it and letting it leak out "sideways," and after only a few months of coaching, people began to notice an authentic difference that was much bigger than simply seeing that he no longer blew up irrationally.

Stefan ultimately received the promotion he wanted, and, perhaps more importantly, he was having more fun at his job than he had in years. He told his coach, "I'm more engaged and I am going the extra mile now—not because I am afraid I'll get into trouble if I don't, but because I really want to." As a commodities trader, Stefan estimated that this increase in his own engagement was literally worth millions to his company. "If I negotiate an extra half cent on a bushel of soybeans, it may not sound like much, but trust me, it's huge."

Standing in this cornerstone calls us to continually focus our attention more broadly. The question "who am I becoming?" gets activated here. From the perspective of evoking transformation, when someone asks, "What should I do?" the answer is often, "I don't know. Who do you want to be? Who do you want to become?" When Stefan came to coaching, he asked, "What do I need to do to get my promotion?" Instead of telling him the right boxes to check off, his coach wisely pointed him to shifting who he was *being* at a very fundamental level. And that is what worked.

Human beings are incredibly complex and, as with all complex systems, share three aspects: one, they are emergent and ever-developing, not static and fixed; two, they are nonlinear as opposed to following set rules in a logical and consistent manner; and three, very small changes to the system can have a profound impact. To view ourselves as somehow "completed" or "arrived" does not honor our natural and innate desire and ability for growth and development. To evoke transformation means we understand we are never done, finished, complete, but always moving and changing in unpredictable ways, changed in a moment by something as simple as a new perspective or idea— this is part of what it is to be human.

Like Stefan, we all get trapped in old stories that can keep us stuck. When we evoke transformation, we call forth the human being who exists beneath our stories, helping that person chart a new direction. For example, Carmela came to the CTI Leadership program mourning a ten-year-old divorce. She told her "woe is me" story to anyone who would listen, and sat in the early classroom sessions slumped in her chair, certain that because she had been treated unfairly and abandoned, ten years ago, she could never truly be happy again.

Then, during a physical activity in the course, she shifted. She realized she had an opportunity to choose and step into life, and she came alive. She smiled and played and looked like a completely different woman at the end of the day. Everyone was thrilled she had finally been able to let go of that disempowering story.

But the next day the old Carmela was back, slumping in her chair, nestled into her "poor me" persona, tears running down her face. The leader, committed to evoking transformation, wasn't going to buy it any longer. She said, "Yesterday we saw that you were ready to be done with your old story. I saw it. Everybody else in the group saw it. Most importantly, *you* saw it. So, I'm declaring an official *end* to the old story. No more *poor me!*" Carmela immediately stopped crying and said, "Really? I'm done?" And the leader said (with great conviction), "Yes!"

This turned out to be the final thing Carmela needed to let go of the old story. She had, after all, been wanting to let go of it for years. The conversation with the leader was not the whole story of her transformation, but it was a critical turning point. After that, she committed to finally stepping into the person she was becoming, not the person she had been. Over the next year she lost forty pounds and started the business she'd been dreaming of. Enough, it turned out, was enough, when someone cared enough to evoke transformation in her.

Rupert has two wonderful, high-potential employees working for him. He takes the view that his job as a manager is largely to evoke transformation and so he looks at them through this lens. One of his employees, Marjorie, is on top of the details, has everything covered, and is truly a make-it-happen person. Rupert's focus with her (while holding *all* of the cornerstones in the process) is to help her expand into the lighter side of her personality.

In contrast, his other employee, Ted, is warm, available, and everyone's friend, but he sometimes misses the important details. Here Rupert focuses on how Ted can expand his capacity for details. With both, Rupert is looking for the next place of human development, the gap each person is facing, and the place they can become more, and thus have more of the effectiveness and success they want for themselves.

There is significant scientific proof for the exciting idea that the brain demonstrates "neuroplasticity." That is, it's more adaptable than we have previously thought, and it can—and does—change with effort and intention. As neuroplasticity expert Norman Doidge points out, there is substantial evidence we can indeed rewire our own brains with our thoughts.

There is a common saying in neuroscience: "Neurons that fire together, wire together." First coined by Donald Hebb, a Canadian neuropsychologist, this axiom reminds us that every experience, thought, feeling, and physical sensation triggers thousands of neurons, which form a neural network. When you repeat an experience over and over, the brain learns to trigger the same neurons each time.

The more a network is used, the stronger it becomes. We have trillions of possible neural connections in our brains. Some of them have wired strongly into habits and behaviors that are effective, and some have wired into limiting beliefs and strategies that are not. And many exist simply as pure potential.

Because the default in our brain is to go with the networks that are most developed, it is difficult to change without focused, supported, intentional effort. Holding the cornerstone of evoke transformation can help bring this sort of focus and support, literally helping the brain rewire itself for greater effectiveness.

Additionally, one of the keys to neuroplasticity is novelty. Things that are new or unexpected get our attention and cause a release of a chemical in the brain that makes new neural connections possible. By evoking transformation, we stretch out of our comfort zone and take risks; we don't just do what we are already doing a little bit better. If we think of evoking transformation, it pushes us toward the kind of expansive thinking that can lead to an aha moment of clarity, a feeling of something new being opened before us.

Standing in the cornerstone of evoking transformation calls us to focus on creating new neural networks that lead to more resonant, effective, fulfilling lives. Over time, through commitment, support, practice, and reflection, those *aha* moments of clarity can become dominant neural pathways, and what was once a challenge will become commonplace.

Tips and Tools for Cornerstone Four: Evoke Transformation

1) A Few Things to Think About
- Think about this powerful saying: "Trust your dreams and doubt your doubts." What does it mean to you and how can you encourage others to do the same?
- There are some powerful and challenging questions in this cornerstone that are well worth exploring, such as:
  ○ What in your life needs to die, or what do you need to let go of?
  ○ What are you tolerating?
  ○ What would you do if you knew you could not fail?

2) A Few Simple Things to Do in your Day-to-Day Life
- Healer and teacher Caroline Myss once said, "We evolve at the rate of the tribe we're plugged into." Surround yourself

with those who are also committed to growing and evolving, and who nourish and feed your best, biggest self. On your journey, be willing to let go of the friends who may not be the friends who meet you now.

- Encourage people to expand their range of possibilities, leaning into what's possible, not predictable. Dare to ask, What else? and How big? Hold dreams for other people until they are ready to claim them and live them for themselves.
- When someone asks you what they should do, try responding, "I don't know. Who do you want to be?"
- Challenge yourself to do something new every month, every week, or even every day. Make a habit of being non-habitual. It's easy to get stuck inside our own comfort zone. Drive a new way to work, use your non-dominant hand to eat or brush your teeth, commit to asking provocative questions when you find yourself in a dull conversation. Shake things up. One of our friends likes to ask, "When is the last time you did something for the first time?"

3) Exercises for Developing this Cornerstone
- Create a visual map of your life. What are mountains you see for yourself? Where are the fertile plains, the rivers, the valleys? What territory would you like to explore next?
- It can be really helpful in this cornerstone to see how far you have already come. One way to do this is to create a timeline of your life by breaking things down into seven-year segments and reflect on the major events and growth during each segment. We find it very powerful to put each timeframe on a separate piece of paper and "walk" up to present day, journaling as you go. You can even walk into the future, allowing yourself to imagine what happens next and where you want to be 7, 14, 21 years ahead. After

the walk, look through your notes for themes around growth and transformation. Who have you become and what else is possible?

The Dance of the Four Cornerstones

Pull a thread here and you'll find it's attached to the rest of the world.
~Nadeem Aslam

While we have described the four cornerstones separately, and even provided stories, examples, and ideas for each, the truth is, they aren't singular in nature. Instead of thinking of them like the pillars of a house, perhaps a better way to envision the cornerstones is as a sort of three-dimensional Venn Diagram, all overlapping and interconnecting with each other, distinct and yet crucial to the whole, or as we will explore in Chapter Seven, the bedrock of a lake.

In a very real way, the cornerstones themselves provide a wonderful example of integration. We differentiate each in order to understand and honor its particular gift. But we don't really live or use them separately. For example, when we encourage a child to follow her dreams, we are holding them naturally creative, resourceful, and whole to know inside what they themselves want, honoring that they are a whole person (and not just their good math score), dancing in this moment with what they are longing for and care about, and even evoking transformation as we encourage them to reach for the stars.

When we lead by focusing on development, growth, and mentoring, seeing the potential in others in our organization, encouraging them to reach, aspire, and surprise themselves to reach new heights, we are also holding and honoring these cornerstones.

Nothing in life is really separate, but sometimes concepts need to be understood as distinct before we can use them in the most powerful way. This is the challenge and the joy of being Co-Active. It calls us not just to do one thing, but to stand in (as best we can) all four cornerstones as the fundamental way we navigate our lives: pillars of strength and stability in an uncertain world.

As we mentioned at the beginning of this chapter, each of the four cornerstones can help with differentiation, linkage, or both. Taken together, they provide a map and a guide for a powerfully integrated life.

Chapter Six

The Power of a Designed Alliance

People are lonely because they build walls instead of bridges.
~Joseph F. Newton

Sharon, a high-level manager at a US company, was facing yet another meeting with a particularly difficult client. Although an experienced project team leader, considered by her work group and manager to have excellent skills and cultural awareness, this European group had her baffled. "We never seem to make much progress when we are together," Sharon reflected. "No matter how carefully I gather input and shape the agenda, petty issues always seem to take us off track. I'm generally pretty good at facilitating—but I just can't seem to get us aligned and clicking together no matter what I do. All I can think is that it's a cultural difference I am not navigating very well."

Unfortunately, Sharon's scenario is all too familiar—and not just in the business world. Even when we carefully shape the agenda and bring all our relationship and communication skills to the table, too often it simply doesn't go the way we had imagined, leaving the parties involved frustrated and defeated instead of motivated and engaged. In this chapter, we'll explore another aspect of the Co-Active model that can make a huge difference: the consciously *designed alliance,* a powerful and highly useful tool for increasing effectiveness in business and in life.

In Co-Active coaching, the designed alliance serves as a container for the coaching relationship, providing a mutually created set of explicit agreements and understandings about how coaching will proceed. In the coaching context, a designed alliance typically covers things such as an agreement to hold confidentiality, an understanding of the scope and focus of the

100

overall coaching, and timing and cost of sessions, as well as subtler aspects including how much the client wants to be challenged and how they want to be held accountable.

And, like all parts of the Co-Active model, the consciously designed alliance is so much more than a structure for coaching. The process of consciously and intentionally designing alliances in our lives provides yet another path to integration. We often sacrifice a relationship because we don't want the same things and don't see the world the same way. Designing an alliance gives us a container for the relationship so we can work out conflict while maintaining connection. This is one of the simplest and best ways to build positive bridges with others (linkage) while honoring our own individuality and needs (differentiation), thus leading to integration.

In this chapter, we'll look at what it means to consciously design an alliance, and how this can help us integrate on all levels—with individuals, groups, and ourselves.

What Is a Consciously Designed Alliance?

To Design: To consciously create; to intend for a definite purpose; to plan and fashion artistically or skillfully.

An Alliance: A formal agreement to cooperate for specific purposes, a merging of efforts or interests; to be allied.

We have many alliances in our lives, places where we merge our efforts or interests. We have alliances with organizations we work for or with; we have alliances as families and in romantic relationships; we have alliances with religious institutions, schools, and community organizations. We have alliances with our friends and on sports teams, and as neighbors or coworkers. Some of these meet the definition of "formal agreements to cooperate for specific purposes" and some exist in the realm of assumptions and expectations, never formally or consciously stated.

In day-to-day life, most of us don't tend to think of designing an alliance. Instead, we create agendas or rules to control (most typically a one-sided process), or simply let things go forth without intention or focus. When our alliances are shaped unconsciously they may be lopsided, favoring one party over another, or not including the needs or talents of an individual or group. Without a designed alliance, a relationship is often not as effective as it could be, or the parties involved may not be able to *integrate*—that is, participate in a way that allows for both differentiation (their own needs are identified and met, and each can offer their unique gifts and talents) and linkage (the duo or group's needs and goals are served).

Consciously and intentionally designing an alliance, on the other hand, upholds and engages the challenge and creativity of figuring out how everyone involved can best bring what they have to the table, get what they need, and make some project or process move forward together, thus exemplifying the power and possibility of integration in action. Designing an alliance is, by nature, a collaborative process, allowing for flexibility and negotiation. (A one-way set of rules is not a designed alliance, even if people agree to them.)

As human beings, we have an unfortunate tendency to interact in our relationships based on assumptions of what others are thinking, feeling, and wanting. This isn't an individualized character flaw; it's a deeply ingrained human tendency. Intentionally designing an alliance is a way to bring assumptions into the open for discussion. There's a great story told by Jerry B. Harvey called "The Road to Abilene" that illustrates the importance of this nicely.

On a hot afternoon visiting in Coleman, Texas, a family is comfortably playing dominoes on a porch, until the father-in-law suggests that they take a trip to Abilene [53 miles north] for dinner.

The wife says, "Sounds like a great idea." The husband, despite having reservations because the drive is long and hot, thinks that his preferences must be out-of-step with the group and says, "Sounds good to me. I just hope your mother wants to go." The mother-in-law then says, "Of course I want to go. I haven't been to Abilene in a long time."

The drive is hot, dusty, and long. When they arrive at the cafeteria, the food is as bad as the drive. They arrive back home four hours later, exhausted.

One of them dishonestly says, "It was a great trip, wasn't it?" The mother-in-law says that, actually, she would rather have stayed home, but went along since the other three were so enthusiastic. The husband says, "I wasn't delighted to be doing what we were doing. I only went to satisfy the rest of you." The wife says, "I just went along to keep you happy. I would have had to be crazy to want to go out in the heat like that." The father-in-law then says that he only suggested it because he thought the others might be bored.

The group sits back, perplexed that they together decided to take a trip which none of them wanted. They each would have preferred to sit comfortably, but did not admit to it when they still had time to enjoy the afternoon.

Actor Henry Winkler once said, "Assumptions are the termites of relationships." One reason we allow assumptions to erode and even destroy our connections is because it's easier for the brain to run on its own assumptions rather than be challenged to stretch and grow—it simply takes less energy to follow a well-worn habitual path than to stay open to new ways of thinking. This once again points to the need for intentionality. An intentionally designed alliance gives everyone the chance to openly discuss their desires without dictating the way it must be, or capitulating to what they think others want. It also shakes up the status quo by giving people the space to voice their assumptions and then choose accordingly.

In addition to being *intentional* rather than *accidental*, the designed alliance has another key component that makes it more than just a friendship or connection. The designed alliance is *about* something. In other words, there is something at stake we are designing our alliance around. In coaching, the stake is the client's growth and development, and the alliance is designed around that. In a meeting, the designed alliance could be around a shared stake of making the best use of everyone's skill and ability, or moving a particular project forward. In a business, the designed alliance might be around the stake of the organization's mission and vision. And in a family, the designed alliance might be about supporting each other and having fun.

It's important that the stake be compelling and relevant to all the parties involved in designing the alliance. If it's not, either a compelling shared stake needs to be discovered or created, or the people involved need to look to see if the project or goal is something they really wish to be involved with.

Karen had this to say about the importance of the stake: "My wedding vows with my husband Henry were the foundation of a lifetime together, and we wrote them with that in mind. We wanted to create a set of promises and commitments that would hold us for our entire lives, with a shared stake of continual personal growth and partnership in bringing transformation to the world. With this stake to design around, we can navigate the storms that come, and keep discovering what will best serve our alliance.

"When I think of my other powerful designed alliances: at work, with my family, even in my individual friendships, there is always something at stake that is larger than my smaller needs and wants. While I still get to ask for what I want and need, I love looking beyond that to what is needed for the larger purpose that the alliance is designed around, the stake."

By the way, the idea of having a compelling stake is not only critical to the designed alliance, it is a powerful perspective in and of itself. Without a stake, we're just sort of hanging out, letting life happen. We tend to do things reflexively, responding as things come our way. A stake calls us to ask, "for the sake of what?" and a life where there is a stake for much of what we do is vibrant, dynamic, intentional, and alive!

We also believe the most powerful designed alliances also take into account the Co-Active nature of human beings. Ideally, the alliance looks at both the *being* and the *doing*, not only addressing what needs to be done, but who we want to be while doing it. While we are generally pretty good at figuring out what needs to be done, we tend to spend less time reflecting on a deeper lever, asking such questions as, "How do we want to treat each other?" Being conscious and purposeful about our actions and intentions has a way of bringing out the best in people, rather than simply allowing individuals to devolve to their particular defaults—which is especially common under stress. Thus a designed alliance that includes being is a tool for helping us stay in a creative rather than a reactive state.

Ann realized how easy it is to forget the how in the middle in a recent video project. "We were very intentional about *what* needed to get done, but completely neglected to talk about *how* we worked together. After I sent my client the project overview and script, they returned it to me completely rewritten, without letting me know their thinking behind the changes. I found myself lost in terms of how I moved forward, and also a bit resentful that they had changed my words. As I debated how to move forward, it hit me that we had never talked about the process of working together. As a writer, I had the assumption I would receive clear feedback so that I could make the changes. As the client, they had the assumption it was open for their input. But we had never discussed this! Our lack of attention to the how cost us critical project time and made things bumpier than they needed to be."

Lastly, the designed alliance is not a one-time, static agreement. Rather, it is alive, dynamic, and can (we might even say *should*) be ever-changing. For example, early on as coauthors of this book, we had a very focused and intentional conversation in the beginning where we explored many aspects of both the *being* and *doing* of the writing and editing process. This ranged from a clear timeline for the process to the way we each wanted to give and receive feedback. And then we continually redesigned as needed, making a point to check in on both structure and process as we went. Holding the designed alliance as supportive and flexible helped us stay both focused *and* connected in relationship as the book.

Thus, a powerful designed alliance includes these four aspects:

- It is consciously and *intentionally* created, taking into account the needs, opinions, and perspectives of the parties involved;
- It is focused around a *stake* the parties are aligned on;
- It is Co-Active in nature, including both *doing* and *being*; and
- It is *flexible* and dynamic, able to provide structure but also change over time as needed.

The designed alliance might be a simple verbal agreement, or it can be a formal contract with all parties officially signing off. As leaders and coaches, we have seen many powerful designed alliances over the years, and some are so subtle as to be even somewhat implicit. And yet, it seems no matter how big or small the issues, the process of open discussion tends to support the stake and empower both parties more fully than those instances where the alliances are somewhat tacit in nature.

Remember Sharon from our opening story, who couldn't make progress with her European client's team? She decided to use the tool of designing the alliance in her next meeting. She did this by taking time at the beginning not only to review the agenda (as she typically would, before quickly getting on with the business at hand), but also to talk openly with all participants about how they wanted the meeting to go, both in terms of what needed to be accomplished as well as how to approach the work and to be with each other.

She was amazed to find out that others were as frustrated as she was by the sidetracking over small details, and once this was brought into the open without pointing fingers, they were able to design an alliance around focusing on the top three agenda items. One person cheerfully and humorously appointed himself the "focus tracker" and committed to pointing out when things were getting derailed. Others asked for a slightly longer non-working lunch so that they had time to get to know the American team better. And all agreed to honor the classic principle of "assume positive intent" in their working relationship with each other.

Sharon came away from the meeting not only feeling much more satisfied about the work that was accomplished, but also connected to her European client group in real and authentic ways. "I can't believe how much we got done and how much fun we had," she shared. "I could tell people were more patient with each other and not reacting as much. And having Marco volunteer to keep us on track ended up being a riot, because he had such a funny way of shaking his head sadly and waggling his finger when we got into the usual petty details. Everyone laughed, we got back on track, and had plenty of time for a longer lunch for once."

The Designed Alliance and the Four Cornerstones of the Co-Active Model

Today we are faced with the preeminent fact that, if civilization is to survive, we must cultivate the science of human relationships... the ability of all peoples, of all kinds, to live together, in the same world, at peace.
~Franklin D. Roosevelt

Ideally, the Co-Active designed alliance doesn't work alone, but rather rests on and enhances the cornerstones of the Co-Active model, as follows:

1) Seeing people as **naturally creative, resourceful, and whole.** When we don't view someone naturally creative, resourceful, and whole, it is often because we feel we need to take care of them, anticipate their needs, and take all the responsibility in a relationship. Seeing others as naturally creative, resourceful, and whole is necessary to the process of designing an alliance. We have to trust that whatever challenges arise, we can work it out, even if strong emotions come up in the process. We don't have to problem-solve or take all the responsibility. In fact, when we try to fix everything, we miss the true potential of relationships, which is the process of being in the conversation and allowing it to transform us.

2) Dance in this Moment. As we mentioned above, designing an alliance is, by its very nature, an ongoing and emergent process, flexing and developing as circumstances and people change. Standing on the cornerstone of dance in this moment is a critical part of the process, and a bit of a paradox. We want to honor what has been agreed upon in the past, while ever aware that it may or may not continue to serve us as we move forward. People change, circumstances change. The cornerstone of dance in this moment reminds us not to get too attached to the way things are, but instead to allow for things to develop and unfold and be redesigned as needed — consciously and intentionally.

3) Focus on the whole person. In terms of the designed alliance, this means allowing and designing not only with the parts we like, but considering and providing space for *all* of what others need, what they ask for, and who they are. It also means designing with the person and not just the role. In other words, while Becky as the president of the company may need one thing, that may or may not include what Becky needs as an individual. And since Becky the person *includes* Becky the president, we start with the person and allow for the role, rather than what is far too common: start with the role and perhaps later, if time allows, ask about the person.

This cornerstone also calls us to move beyond the assumption that the other person or people are like us and want what we want. Focusing on the whole person reminds us to make room for human complexity when we are designing the alliance.

4) Evoke transformation. Consciously designing an alliance takes intention and the courage to discuss things openly. At times this may mean friction and dissatisfaction come up that were buried under a patina of politeness or assumptions. Just like the sand in the oyster that creates the pearl, this discomfort usually signifies a significant opportunity for growth. When we consciously design an alliance from a place of evoking transformation, sometimes we have to face things that are uncomfortable, and in facing them openly, we grow, develop, and transform.

Designing an Alliance with Another Person

Relationships are part of the vast plan for our enlightenment.
~Marianne Williamson

Ah, the complexity of living, working, or creating with someone else! At its best, it can be a synergistic dance of delight; at its worst, it can feel like hell on earth. Hundreds of books have been written over the years about how to get along with others, and there are endless theories, models, and ideas. It's a vast and fascinating field, and we don't presume by any means to offer the final, definitive answer here. That being said, we have seen again and again that the intentional act of designing an alliance with another for the sake of a shared stake is powerful, effective, and can transform difficult relationships into productive ones.

All our relationships—whether at work, school, home, or anywhere else—bring up things that are difficult at times. It would be nice (maybe) to think that only our "non-professional" interactions involve emotions and challenges, but we all know this isn't true. We can't help it. All humans have emotions, and things that trigger us, and part of our evolution is to learn to work with these emotions and triggers and still stay connected and get the job done. In fact, as Marianne Williamson says, it may well be that this is not just the challenge in relationships—it's the very reason we are connected to one another in the first place.

An intentionally designed alliance gives us the opportunity to stay connected and to go deeper. Instead of throwing up our hands and walking away when things get uncomfortable, we have a tool for staying in the conversation. Our discomfort becomes a signal to bring our own needs or perspective to the table for discussion and, if needed, a design or redesign of the alliance. Again, an intentionally designed alliance points us to integration because we can honor our differentiation and still link rather than feel we need to choose one or the other, which is what often happens without one.

Stefan found himself at an impasse with his ex-wife. Their teenage son was not keeping up the GPA he needed in order to participate on the lacrosse team, and Stefan was certain it was all his former wife's fault. "I know she lets him get away with not studying," he fumed. "He's a great athlete and I know he's capable of getting much better grades." Stefan felt there was nothing he could do since his son was only with him part-time and he "knew" how his ex-wife would be about taking a firmer stand.

Through taking the CTI coaching classes, Stefan was introduced to the idea of the designed alliance, and he realized that there was actually something he could do: he could take responsibility and create an alliance with his ex. "I was giving all my power away and being a victim," he said. "I started seeing that maybe it wasn't true that there was nothing I could do. I wasn't sure it would work, but I thought, *what the heck, it's worth a try, and it's good practice!"*

Instead of going into the conversation defensive and feeling defeated as he had in the past, the first thing he did was to say outright that he wanted to find common ground and a plan in which they both could align, and that he wanted to hear what she wanted, too. From there, he reflected upon their shared commitment to and shared stake in their son and his academic and athletic success. "That alone was transformational," he shared. "I have tended to come from blame because I was so frustrated. Of course that put her on edge, and we never got anywhere."

When they were able to see they both wanted the same thing, the planning became much easier, and they realized the need to involve their son and his coach in similar conversations. "It was amazing," Stefan said. "We got everyone on board and instead of each of us feeling defensive and misunderstood, we became this team, aligned around Josh having a great senior year. It took away so much of my stress over his future. And he actually pulled it off and even got a lacrosse scholarship to college."

As Stefan saw, designing an alliance is an opportunity to take responsibility in a relationship. It's easy to complain and/or walk away, but when we do, we miss both an opportunity to grow and a chance to stay connected.

A similarly powerful example came from our friend Carrie. She heard that a neighbor was battling cancer, and wanted to do something to help. "Like most people," she reported, "I felt a bit paralyzed at first. I didn't know what he and his wife wanted or needed. I didn't want to feel like an intruder, but I also wanted to do *something*." She and her husband Dean decided to see if they could use the tool of designing an alliance with the couple. "It took some courage, but we just decided to go over and be completely open. We didn't say 'let's design an alliance,' but that's what we intended."

Instead of just asking what they could do, Carrie and Dean used the Co-Active model and asked their neighbors first how they wanted this time to be, and what kind of relationship they wanted with their neighbors. "We told them that what we wanted was to be helpful, but also respect their space. They were honestly relieved to have an out in the open discussion, and we felt so honored to be included in this precious time in their lives."

Each relationship—whether it be work partnerships, parent and child, romantic partners, and so on—is different, but regardless of the specifics, there are some basic things to cover when consciously designing an alliance and these include:

Consciously and *intentionally* have a conversation about your alliance.

Look at and find some sort of alignment on a *stake*. What is important about being together or working on a particular project or issue? What is the purpose of your relationship at this time, in this context?

Include both *doing* and *being* aspects. What do we want to accomplish and who do we want to be together while doing so?

Be sure to honor *flexibility* with an ongoing commitment to design and redesign as needed. You may have one overall designed alliance that covers your relationship in general, and several others that are created for specific projects or events.

Designing an Alliance with Another Person

A Few Things to Think About
- When you are frustrated, worried, or feeling disconnected in any relationship, this may be a clue that it's time to design or redesign. Instead of going to confrontation,

avoidance, or even despair, ask yourself: What is it I actually want right now? What is important here? What could I design with this person?

- Notice the assumptions you have about the people you are in relationship with, both personally and professionally. You might want to develop a habit of asking yourself, a la the spiritual teacher Byron Katie, "Is this assumption true? Do I absolutely, positively, know it to be true? What if it weren't true?"

A Few Simple Things to Do in your Day-to-Day Life

- Ask those around you what is working or not working for them in your relationship. Tell them you want to design something that works for *both* of you.
- In your relationships that are more about doing, start asking questions like, "How do we want to be/stay connected while we do this?" In your relationships that are more about being, start asking, "What would we like to accomplish together?"

Exercises for Designing an Alliance with Another Person

- Follow the steps that Stefan modeled in the story above:
  1. Let go of blaming and being "right". This might honestly be the hardest part, but it can help to remember it is for the sake of something bigger. It's simply not possible to create a designed alliance from a position of being right.
  2. Find a shared stake.
  3. Design actions—ideally being and doing—around that stake.
- Use the following "Relationship Engine" process:

Step 1: Take Responsibility. Take responsibility for your part in the situation while holding others accountable for their part.

- How have you contributed to the current situation?
- Have you been impatient? Judgmental?
- What are the assumptions you have made up?
- Where have you taken things personally?
- Where have you been practicing "problem spotting"? rather than "value spotting"?
- What seems important to the other person?
- How would you like things to shift?

Step 2: Choose. Consider a range of options rather than defaulting to the obvious or expedient.
- What ideally do you really want?
- Are you willing to do something about that? If so, what?
- What is already in place to support your desired outcome?
- What are several options?
  IMPORTANT NOTE: Your course of action may, BUT DOES NOT HAVE TO, include a conversation with the other person.
- Choose the course of action that most resonates.

Step 3: Align. Select a course of action that provides the most benefit to you and others involved.
- How will you benefit from your chosen course of action?
- How will others benefit?
- How does your choice align with your values?

Step 4: Commit.
- What are the steps you need to take to make your course of action real?
- What will you do and by when will you do it?

Designing an Alliance with a Group or Team

Politeness is the poison of collaboration.
~Edwin Land

As we saw in Sharon's story, the designed alliance is not just for one-on-one relationships, but can be a powerful tool for groups as well. Designing an alliance gives us a chance to shape things collaboratively for maximum positive impact for all concerned, leading to both engagement and productivity. Generally, however, we tend to operate somewhere on a continuum between rigidly planning all the details in order to keep things under control, or "winging it" without structure so that anything goes. In the first case, individual needs and ideas can't blossom, and in the second, often nothing gets done.

Designing an alliance with a group means airing assumptions and being willing to speak the truth in order to trust that there is room for our contributions and concerns. As a leader, it calls us to intentionally create a space for this possibility within each meeting or gathering. Darcy, an educational consultant, gave us a wonderful example of this skill in her work with teachers at a summer camp. "First, since the teachers were team teaching, I had them design an alliance amongst themselves," she shared. "From there, I gave them a template to use to design with the classroom on Day One. I got to sit in on two of the different camps when they were designing with the kids and it was fascinating. I noticed a big shift from other years in that the students felt they were a part of the course and that their voices were heard. They worked together to create a class objective and also to create agreements around what was needed to have camp be a safe and courageous space. We all noticed a big movement away from business as usual in that there was a sense of co-creation in the classroom as opposed to teachers dictating down to the students. The students were much more engaged and comfortable with the instructors, and the way they spoke up showed it."

Designing an alliance with a group or team is not the same as simply cooperating. If you do an Internet search for teamwork, you will find hundreds of quotations on the importance of subsuming your own individual needs to the needs of the group. As the saying goes, "There is no "I" in team!" (Although Michael Jordan famously retorted, "Yes, but there is in 'win.'") Again, designing an alliance allows us to bring our differentiated selves—the "I"—to link with the group or team, the "we."

In honoring the I, we also need to be sure our own values align with the values of the group or organization. Joining or employment is the beginning of the relationship, part of the design, and this is the first place we need to be clear as individuals whether the stake is something we care about or not. For example, someone with a high value of service and making a difference may feel fundamentally unaligned with an organization whose sole purpose is profit. It's important to recognize this; alignment is not something we can fake!

There is no one right way to design a group alliance. As we mentioned above, it can range from very formal and structured to somewhat informal (more like a check-in), but as a practical manner, designing an alliance with a group might look something like this:

1) Consciously and *intentionally* create the time and space to design together at the beginning of the enterprise or gathering. When we don't hold ourselves as responsible to design the alliance, the particles (the agenda or to-do list) design it for us.

2) Align on the *stake*, the purpose for being together, the outcomes. Why are you there, why are you together?

3) Include both *doing* and *being* aspects of working together. What do we want to accomplish and who do we want to be together while doing so?

4) Be up-front and explicit about *flexibility*. Make sure everyone knows things can and will be redesigned as needed.

Designing an Alliance with a Group or Team

A Few Things to Think About
- People often get caught up in an urgency mindset that keeps them from taking the time to design before diving in to the agenda. Notice your own beliefs around this, and start collecting new evidence for the effectiveness of taking time to create an alliance first. As the saying goes, it is often most helpful to "go slow to go fast."
- In the groups you are in, ask yourself, are we the kind of group that allows for people to have their own needs?

A Few Simple Things to Do in your Day-to-Day Life
- Start noticing when the group may be drifting off track and be willing to name it and see what can be designed instead.
- Practice asking for 100% of what you want, 100% of the time, while being available to negotiate the difference between your 100% and the 100% of the other group members.
- For any group event, from business meeting to family vacation, create a stake that will orient the group.

Exercise for Designing an Alliance with a Group or Team
- Try these questions for designing a meeting alliance:
  - What would great communication between group members look like?
  - How does each individual empower the group?
  - How does the group empower each individual?
  - What would a good group dynamic look like?

Designing an Alliance with the Different Parts of Ourselves

You must first get along with yourself before you can get along with others.
~Anthony D'Angelo

While it might sound odd to think about designing an alliance with oneself, the truth is we are often in conflict with different aspects of our own being. On the one hand, we know we want to relax and enjoy life, and on the other, we want to accomplish things and make a name for ourselves. We want to be warm and easy to connect with, and we want to hold the line on productivity and profit. We want to go out and we want to stay in. Most introverts have some extrovert in them, and most extroverts need alone time too. We are not one thing. We are complexity itself.

We are actually designed to be integrated, to have differentiated parts of ourselves link and work together. Think of how our body moves through life—heart pumping, lungs breathing, each organ doing what is needed, playing its role in the whole. As an illustration, Ann once went to the eye doctor because she realized she needed glasses for reading. Instead, the doctor advised her to remove one contact lens, leaving her right eye to see distance and her left to see close objects. It felt odd for about a day, and then Ann's eyes adjusted, seamlessly working together to provide both aspects of vision such that she doesn't even notice which eye is doing what. Differentiated, and linked, in an alliance around helping Ann to see!

While our physical body discerns how best to work together for the good of the whole, other parts of our being aren't always as cooperative. And one of the ways we get most dis-integrated from ourselves is by honoring one part at the expense of others. One example often comes up in coaching when a client is helped first to identify values and then to focus on increasing the satisfaction level of each important value. This isn't an easy task. To honor one key value is not an issue—we do that all the time. But to look at our top five or six values and then to figure out how to honor *all* of them? Well, that's quite possibly the work of a lifetime! If I honor my value for ease, how do I honor my value for security? My value for play seems in conflict with my value for achievement. What do I do? Which do I fulfill? Holding all parts of ourselves as important is certainly a challenge at best!

This is often where we get stuck and even at war with ourselves. Those of us who calibrate toward freedom (which can take us, at its worst, to chaos) tend to resent the parts of ourselves that want some sort of secure ground to stand on. Those of us who go the other way and are more comfortable with structure (leading us, at its worst, to rigidity) can have a hard time letting even a tiny bit of our own freak flags fly. And yet, as we saw in Chapter Three, we are all both—designed to hold dual energies and challenged to integrate ourselves into a differentiated and linked whole.

Designing an alliance with ourselves is a powerful way to do this. It's less of a step-by-step procedure and more of a consistent perspective to hold and come from, but if it were a linear process, it might look something like this:

1) I consciously and *intentionally* choose to create an internal alliance. When I begin to see the value and challenge of knowing and honoring *all* aspects of my being, not just some, I am called to explore who I am and what I need as a whole person. This may mean being willing to acknowledge parts of myself that have been shut down or devalued, as well as those that are dominant and strong.

2) As I connect more deeply with parts of myself, I often begin to realize there is something big at *stake*. In this case, it is the biggest thing of all—our "one wild and precious life," as the poet Mary Oliver so eloquently states.

3) I honor both my *"being"* aspects and my *"doing"* aspects. When I design an alliance with myself, I need to look at both what I want to accomplish and create, as well as who I want to be and how I want to feel while doing so.

4) I understand the importance of *flexibility*. When I know I am always a work in progress, I see that I can redesign as and when needed. I can either judge and self-criticize when I fail (as I certainly will from time to time), or I can forgive myself, look to what I learned and what I need, and try again. I can also remain open to my own evolution and changing desires; what I want in this moment may not be what I want next year, or even next week.

In practice, designing an alliance with ourselves is a habit or perspective that tends to get stronger and more accessible with practice. Monica is a wonderful example of this. A leader in the business sector as well as a creative artist, a few years ago she began to be aware of competing tugs on her attention. She was feeling unsatisfied and stressed in her job, and the newly developing artist part of her was saying, "Just quit! Be free!" But she was also aware that there were many aspects to the work that she valued, enjoyed, and wanted to master. The achiever part of her was saying, "Look how far you've come as a manager already. There is so much more you can accomplish if you focus on your career and move ahead!" At first, she found herself listening to one voice or the other. She'd tilt toward quitting and then tilt back toward focusing on her career. This was a distressing and even painful state to be in.

A friend who was trained in the Co-Active model suggested she get these parts of herself in the same room, so to speak. As she stopped and listened to the competing voices, she began to realize that it truly wasn't an either/or proposition. Her free and creative self had real, undeniable needs for self-expression and playing outside of boundaries. And her structured, achievement-oriented self had a need for accomplishment and challenge. Over time, she found ways to gain more freedom and space within her job as a manager, while taking on new tasks that were challenging and exciting. For example, she began to take more leadership in her job, rather than waiting to be asked, and also began conversations with her manager about growth opportunities. She also connected with a group of people focused on creative expression so that the artist side of her had a regular outlet and focus for its needs.

We have a tendency to believe that the dominant emotion at the time is the capital "T" Truth rather than simply one note of our orchestra of emotions (which are sometimes discordant). There is freedom in realizing that however we are feeling in the moment is a part of our being—true and important—but not the whole truth. Therefore we have a choice, and ultimately a challenge, to bring all our aspects into some sort of harmony. And harmony is a wonderful metaphor for integration. Each instrument holds its own note, and they come together into something powerful and rich.

When we design an alliance by saying to each part of ourselves, "you are important to me, you deserve to have a voice," it brings harmony to our spirit and lessens the negative self-talk we are all susceptible to at times. This harmony is healing, profound, and ultimately quite practical, because we are never more effective than when not at war with ourselves. When our choices are based on an attempt to honor all the aspects of our being rather than prescriptions for what we should do, or others' ideas of fulfillment, we can truly soar. And when we know that we are complex and ever-emergent, we can fearlessly try to see whether something fulfills us or not. As Ann likes to say, "Life is a joyous experiment—be your own guinea pig!"

Designing an Alliance with Different Aspects of Yourself

A Few Things to Think About

- Heighten your awareness around your own enjoyment. Notice if what you are doing (or are being asked to do) makes your energy go up, or sends it down. This is your best cue that something may be missing, needed, or out of alignment with some core part of your being.
- Pay attention to the words *always* and *never* and *should* when referencing or thinking about yourself. Be curious about what is prompting these absolutes.
- Ask yourself, what is no longer true about me? Do I need a new alliance with myself because I have changed and grown?

A Few Simple Things to Do in your Day-to-Day Life

- Practice speaking to yourself as you would to a dear friend or well-loved child.
- It's okay to take care of yourself—an integrated person is calmer, more creative, easier to be around, and ultimately more effective. When you honor the needs of your whole self, there is more available for others (plus you are a great role model!).
- Notice the experience you're having in the moment. Know that how you are feeling is real, and a legitimate part of you. It's not necessarily *all* of you, but it isn't bad or wrong.

An Exercise for Designing an Alliance with the Different Aspects of Yourself

- As we saw in Monica's example above, we all have parts of ourselves that feel on the surface like they are in conflict with each other. Here's a creative way to work with this:
  1. Take a piece of paper and brainstorm these aspects by putting them around the edges, leaving the middle

blank. We each have our own cast of inner characters, but some titles might be:

   i. My achiever

   ii. My free spirit

   iii. My responsible self

   iv. My creative self

   v. My wise self

2. In the middle, put the issue you are working on, or, if there is no issue present and you just want to explore, put your full self. Draw a line to the center from each cast member. On this line, write their perspective on the issue or on you (as your full self). See what awareness opens up for you.

3. You can also draw lines connecting each of the aspects to each other. On the line, write notes about the designed alliance between these two aspects of yourself. For example, how can the wise self design an alliance with the free spirit?

• For wonderful resources in this area, see CRR Global's Inside Team training or the CTI's work on Captain and Crew.

Designing our Alliance with Life Itself

I live on Earth at present,
and I don't know what I am.
I know that I am not a category.
I am not a thing—a noun.
I seem to be a verb,
an evolutionary process—
an integral function of the universe.
~R. Buckminster Fuller

It may seem odd to think about designing an alliance with life itself, and yet, this is another area that calls us to differentiate and link. If indeed our individual actions and beings resonate as a ripple into the wider universe, with our presence influencing the entire cosmos and vice versa, how do we powerfully connect with that space? How do we hold ourselves as the special, dynamic, unique individuals we are, bringing this uniqueness to the sense of connection with everything?

Jan had this story to share: "I was sitting on my porch drinking tea and watching the animals in my backyard," she said. "The squirrels were playing in the oak trees, the cardinals were building a nest in a dense hedge, there were some wild geese high up overhead, and I was there as well, breathing my breath into the same space. It occurred to me that I was in relationship with all of it—trees, animals, sky, earth.

"As a Co-Active coach, I am a big believer in the designed alliance, and I try to have designed alliances in all areas of my life. So I thought to myself, *What is my alliance here? How can I design with this life unfolding before me?* I realized that it was actually like anything else—if I wasn't intentional, it would be a 'default' alliance, not fully serving anyone. So I sat in stillness and asked the universe what it wanted from me, and it told me it wanted me and other humans to walk on it with dignity and happiness. And it wanted me to stop and pay attention to its delights, just as I had been as I sat with my tea. Then I asked it for what I needed from it, which was to continue cleaning my air, supporting my feet, and delighting me with its beauty. A lovely, peaceful feeling came over me, and I felt connected in a new way to everything around me."

Many of us do have alliances with life and the universe in a way, like Jan, that makes sense to us. For some, it is about living sustainably and we recycle and make decisions about what we eat, buy, or wear as part of this alliance. For others, it might be a connection with energy, a sort of alliance around co-creating life that can even seem somewhat magical. These can be ways of dancing in partnership with all that is, while honoring our own human needs.

Just as with any other designed alliance, there are four elements to hold in mind:

1) Be conscious and intentional about designing the alliance. In this case this could mean looking at what the universe might want and need from us as well as what we want and need from it.
2) Know and honor a stake for the alliance: for example, a sustainable planet.
3) Consider the being and the doing.
4) Design and redesign.

Designing an Alliance with Life

A Few Things to Think About
- Ask yourself, "Who do I want to be as I walk on this earth?" and "What are the assumptions I have about what the earth should do for me?"
- What is the shared stake you personally have with life itself? What can you align around?
- Explore your legacy. What are you here to create or make?

A Few Simple Things to Do in your Day-to-Day Life
- Start a dialogue with life in your journal, meditation or prayers. Ask what it wants from you, and share your own hopes and dreams.
- As you go through your day, heighten your awareness to the messages that are surrounding you. The things that call your attention may point you toward areas for action. For example, are you drawn to stories about animal cruelty but are not currently involved? Perhaps the world needs your efforts there!

An Exercise for Designing an Alliance with Life

* Set aside a full day to be alone in nature. Get as far away from buildings, traffic noise and human-made things as possible. Refrain from doing something active like going for a hike, but instead perhaps slowly stroll as you walk, taking the time to stop, look and listen. Simply be still and present with the natural world around you. Be curious about what is needed from you right now. How can you serve life? How is life serving you?

In Conclusion

Our intention creates our reality.
~Dr. Wayne Dyer

In every area of life, the intentionally designed alliance is a powerful tool. And while you won't necessarily always get what you want by asking for it, your chances will increase exponentially. There's a wonderful story told by the author Thomas Friedman which illustrates this point.

There once was a very religious Jew named Goldberg who wanted to win the lottery. He would go to synagogue every Sabbath and pray: "God, I have been such a pious man all of my life. What would be so bad if I won the lottery?" And the lottery would come, and Goldberg would not win. This went on week after week, month after month. Finally, one Sabbath, Goldberg couldn't take it anymore, and cried out to the Almighty: "God, I have been so good, so observant. What do I have to do to win the lottery?"

And suddenly the heavens parted and the voice of God boomed out: "Goldberg, give me a chance. Buy a ticket."

Too often in life we act like Goldberg, waiting and hoping that life will somehow unfold in a more fulfilling way but not actually buying the ticket. We leave jobs because we're at odds with management or feel undervalued. We suffer through vacations that don't live up to our hopes and dreams. And overall, we far too often resign ourselves to less than ideal situations because "that's just the way it is." While designing an alliance is not a magic wand ensuring a life of perfection, it is a hopeful and valuable tool for shaping things in a way that serves everyone more fully. We might as well buy a ticket and see what happens!

Chapter Seven

The Five Keys To Integration

Perhaps the truth depends on a walk around the lake.
~Wallace Stevens

Imagine your favorite lake. Picture it sparkling with morning light, or covered by fog looking mysterious. Watch the sun rise or set over the water, notice the fish jump and the dragonflies buzz past you. Envision your lake both calm and stormy, and notice the life, aliveness and movement of its waters. Your lake, with all it holds, is a wonderful metaphor for the entire Co-Active model.

Your lake started as a depression in the ground, carved by glaciers or erosion or the shifting restlessness of earth herself. The lakebed, made of bedrock, covered by sand, weeds or dirt, represents the *cornerstones* of the Co-Active model. The cornerstones are always there, holding everything steady and secure.

Now picture the shore, the beaches, the rocks and trees, the way the water laps up and is contained. This represents the *designed alliance* of the Co-Active model, which defines the boundaries, shape, and even the purpose of your lake.

And now look at the water itself. Notice its depth and color. In this metaphor, the water represents what we call the *contexts* of the Co-Active model, which, in this case, we are also calling the "keys to integration." These are:

- Listening
- Intuition
- Curiosity
- Forward the Action/Deepen the Learning
- Self-Management

Like the water in your lake, these contexts are fluid. They blend into each other, work together, and can happen at the same time with no discernable edge or boundary: Listening flows into Intuition, requiring both Self-Management and Curiosity, as we focus on the interplay of Forwarding the Action and Deepening the Learning.

And, just as in a lake there are often cooler spots or places where it becomes shallower and the light reflects differently, one of the contexts may move into sharper focus for a time. We may consciously choose to heighten our Curiosity, or decide we've Deepened the Learning and need to Forward the Action now. Ultimately, though, the five contexts are blended and inseparable. Swimming in them, letting them shape and lift us, creates integration in ourselves, our relationships and our world.

Thus, the lake is held by its bedrock, the *cornerstones*, defined by the shore, a *designed alliance*, and full of water in which to play, the *contexts*. Let's dive into the water and see what's there.

The First Context—Listening

Listening is a magnetic and strange thing, a creative force. The friends who listen to us are the ones we move toward. When we are listened to, it creates us, makes us unfold and expand.
~Karl Menninger

As Menninger so beautifully puts it, truly being listened to allows us to "unfold and expand." So the first water in our lake is the context of **Listening**. We all know it is important to listen, just as we know how much we value those relationships where it is present. We are naturally aware of subtle distinctions in listening, and we say things like "I just love my new friend Rachel. She *really* listens." Given the fact that we talk and (presumably) listen all the time, why is it such a big deal to be actually, authentically listened to? In other words, what's the difference between listening as most people do in day-to-day life, and the kind of listening that has us unfold and expand?

The truth is, we all have the capacity to listen at many levels, from automatic self-referential responses (known as *Level One* in the Co-Active model), to an intense focus on what the other person is saying (what we call *Level Two*) to the ability to hear at a broader level, including what is not being said and even what is present in what we might call "the energetic field" (*Level Three*).

These levels are fascinating not only intuitively, but also from a neuroscience perspective. To begin with, the evolving understanding of the brain indicates we never get completely away from what we know as Level One. If we did, we might not understand anyone at all. This has to do with the fact that many of the neurons in our brain are "multi-modal"—that is, the same ones fire if we do something (like lift a pen), if we watch someone doing something (even if we're not doing it ourselves, the same motor neurons in our own brains fire if someone else lifts a pen), if we imagine something (visualizing ourselves lifting a pen), and if we remember something (recalling when we lifted a pen).

As neuroscientist Jerome Feldman, an expert on how the brain understands language, puts it: "If you cannot imagine someone picking up a glass, you can't understand the meaning of 'someone picked up a glass.'" We have to run an idea through our own experience, effectively "simulating" things in our own brains in order to make them meaningful. In the process, we latch on to places in our experience that connect with what we are being told.

For example, when someone says, "I went to Yellowstone National Park on vacation last week," our brains automatically sort through data to find a connection, a way to make this information personally meaningful. We think of vacations, of mountains, of the geyser "Old Faithful," etc. Without consciously doing so, we are, in effect, asking ourselves, "How can I know this person? How can I understand her experience?"

The challenge with this is that far too often we get stuck in the simulation, in our own "Level One" processing and response. While this is important for a baseline understanding, it only provides our own take on things, and thus keeps us living in assumptions and not really hearing the other person.

In other words, for most people, as Fran Lebowitz once remarked, the opposite of talking isn't listening. The opposite of talking is waiting. Generally we wait for our turn to talk and respond automatically rather than thoughtfully. Our brains give us about 17 seconds to take in information before we need to make it personally meaningful (if you time 17 seconds, you'll find it is about ten words in normal conversation). After that, our brains are looking for their own connection to the topic. Wait, what did you say?

This is compounded by sheer busy-ness and pace of modern life. All manner of information is readily available at our fingertips, so we tend to stay on the surface, not paying full attention to who we are with because we're paying attention to something else, from smart phones to the ubiquitous overhead TVs in public spaces, to our internal to-do lists.

Far too often, our conversations come from an exclusively Level One place and therefore sound like ping-pong matches, with each person simply waiting to hit the conversational ball:

A: I went to Yellowstone last week on vacation.
B: You did? I was there many years ago. It's beautiful. My kids loved Old Faithful.
A: Yeah, well, it's changed a lot in the past few years. You can't even find a place to park by most of the main attractions.
B: We went off-season in the fall. That's the time to go, if you ask me. We always go to the National Parks off-season.
A: Yeah, well, we're stuck to the school schedule, you know.
B: That's why we homeschool. Best way to do it.

And so on. A conversation of sorts (or perhaps two separate conversations!), but when both people are in Level One, not much in the way of connection or understanding is actually happening. Ironically, understanding is most likely what the brain is, on some level, attempting to do by imposing its own meaning and reference points onto the other's experience.

In the Co-Active model, there are additional levels of listening available once we can become aware of our own "Level One" thoughts and reactions and move to a more present, thoughtful engagement with the other person. By adding Levels Two and Three to our listening, our "Level One" provides helpful information and potential insight, a way of understanding while allowing the focus to be, for a time, on the other person.

Level Two and Level Three listening could be thought of as ways to intentionally engage the dual hemispheres of the brain for maximum connection and understanding. Ideally, they operate in concert: Level Two listening providing focused, precise (more left-hemisphere) listening, with Level Three broadening the awareness to a holistic, inclusive, intuitive (more right-hemisphere) way of taking in the information. Skilled Co-Active Coaches dance smoothly between these levels, listening not only to the specific words and ideas, but taking in the emotional content and desires beneath the words, which are sometimes not fully realized by the client themselves. (And here we begin to see how the contexts interrelate. Listening at Levels Two and Three requires, at a minimum, bringing in Self-Management to stop our automatic "me too" reactions and Curiosity to find out more about what the other person is saying. More on those to come!)

Listening at Levels Two and Three is a powerful key to integration, which, as you will recall from Chapter Three, we are defining as the *linkage* of *differentiated* parts. When we are able to *differentiate* our own "Level One" thoughts and desires *and* shift attention to another, we can move "over there" to the other person's world and *link* with them authentically. And we have an impact that is more than emotional—as we mentioned in the chapter on the Cornerstones, the process of having what Dan Siegel calls "collaborative, contingent conversations," which are emotionally attuned and non-directive, builds positive neural connections in the brain.

In other words, when we can differentiate our own experience of Yellowstone National Park, and be aware of our "Level One" opinions and judgments about someone else's trip (and whether they are doing it right or wrong), we can set these opinions and judgments aside and truly seek to understand the other's experience. And thus, we are practicing integration. What's magical about this is that our own world expands as a result. Our own experience of Yellowstone takes on new color because we can also see it through someone else's eyes. Through the integration that occurs as a result of this multilevel listening, each person's experience is expanded.

True listening in the way we are referencing it points ultimately to listening to the *person*, not just the content. There is a great example of this in the delightful 2003 movie *Love Actually*. One of the main characters meets a woman who only speaks Portuguese, while he only speaks English. They manage to connect, and even fall in love, without ever speaking words the other understands until the end. As Ralph Waldo Emerson said, "Who you are speaks so loudly I can't hear what you are saying." When we truly pay attention, the person shines through.

Mary was a practical, determined teacher with a huge heart. She came to a coaching skills class a few years ago determined to learn the "next new thing" that would enable her to sharpen her skills. What she found changed her life. "I never ever realized that I was living almost completely in Level One!" she told us. "I had no idea there was another way. I must have driven everyone around me crazy, but I had *no idea*. I went home after the first day of class with the homework to listen at Levels Two and Three and be aware of my own Level One. Wow. That night at dinner my family had the first real conversation we've had in years. It felt magical! I kept thinking, 'Oh dear, this won't last,' until I realized that I have the power to bring it back at any time by just toning down my own darn Level One a bit!"

The self-development teacher Werner Erhard once said, "What most people do is to ignore people's quality and deal with their garbage. Actually, you should do it the other way around. Deal with who they are and let go of their garbage. Keep interacting with them as if they are God. And every time you get garbage from them, ignore the garbage and go back and interact with them as if they were God." In other words, don't just listen, *listen*.

Key Points

1. Conscious listening at all three levels is a simple and yet powerful way to integrate. First, by becoming aware of our own "Level One" listening, we can *differentiate* our own thoughts, biases, opinions and needs. Then with awareness and intention on Level Two and Three listening, we *link* by moving our attention to another or others.

2. Intentional listening grows our consciousness and expands our world. We are both connected and distinct, and when we truly listen we are able to enter another's world and share their experience, making our own world expand and grow.

3. It's crucial to listen to the *person*, not just the content or problem. Thus, the importance of listening not just at Level Two, to the words, but also at Level Three, to the emotion and the being.

4. True listening is relational, not simply receptive. In other words, we are not simply a passive receptacle for people's words. It is both "Co" and "Active" in nature. We are most able to "unfold and expand" when the other person is responsive, co-creative, and engaged with us.

The Second Context—Intuition

It is always with excitement that I wake up in the morning wondering what my intuition will toss up to me, like gifts from the sea. I work with it and rely on it. It's my partner.
~Jonas Salk

The second context is **Intuition**, our ability to know or sense what is going on without directly being told, or without logical analysis. Intuition enables us to hear what's below the surface and guide the conversation to deeper, more resonant places. It helps us know quickly what needs to happen, whether a person is trustworthy or not, and if an idea "has legs."

Intuition helps us know more deeply what is going on for ourselves and others, what is needed in the moment, and how to get beyond surface conversations to the real heart of the matter. As a key to integration, it helps us know when to make boundaries (differentiate) and how to connect (link). Without intuition, the waters of our lake would be shallow indeed.

But what, exactly, is intuition? While most people would probably agree that it exists, intuition has tended to live in a sort of shadowy netherworld, undefined and mysterious. Psychologist Carl Jung defined it as perception via the unconscious, and made a distinction between those who primarily use intuition versus those who primarily think. This is the polarity view we tend toward as human beings, holding someone as either intuitive or rational, but generally not both.

So why then do we have this as a context, as part of the water of our Co-Active lake, if it is something only some people can do? Well, we hold that intuition isn't just the realm of those individuals who walk more on the "woo-woo" side of things. It's actually rational, explainable, and available to everyone.

The truth is, we all use intuition, although there tends to be little agreement about what it actually *is*. But without a clear understanding, it's difficult to understand exactly how to develop, refine and attune it. Perhaps the problem lies in trying to understand intuition as a thing, as one aspect of our brain or being. What we have seen instead is that intuition is actually a highly complex and interrelated system of processes in the brain and body, a system that is fully accessible—and one that can be further developed and explored—by everyone.

This sophisticated system of below-conscious-awareness consists of at least these aspects, and probably more:

1) Context. A participant in a coaching-skills training that one of us led several years ago was convinced she had no intuition. We challenged her to go home to practice anyway. When she came back the next day, she said, "I went home with no interest in doing my homework, so I worked on a grant proposal instead. In the middle of it, as I found myself effortlessly slotting in numbers and responding to outcome questions, I realized that what you are calling intuition, I just call common sense."

This is understandable from a brain perspective. One aspect of intuition, it turns out, is contextual, or domain-specific; i.e., contingent on how much experience we have in a certain area. For example, we both have been coaching and teaching for years and have thousands of hours of experience with human beings. Relationships, leadership, growth, misery, joy—we have truly heard it all. This is part of each of our coaching intuition systems, data sets we draw on unconsciously. Our brains map patterns and look for connections automatically, and because there is so much to draw on, they tend to provide insight with tremendous subtlety and accuracy.

But if you asked either of us to predict what new fashion trends will emerge next year, we'd be at a loss, because neither one of us has much experience in that arena. If we had to buy a clothing line for a department store, we'd have to rely almost completely on rational analysis—a slow and painful process. On the other hand, if you assigned the same task to one of our friends, who worked as a retail buyer for 20 years, he'd make his selections immediately and intuitively, based on his understanding of which items would and wouldn't sell.

What's interesting about this sort of intuition is that the rational-processing part of the brain looks for reasons to justify its instincts, but subtle research using brain scans shows that we actually decide first, and then look for evidence that we are right. Intuition rules!

Not surprisingly, this aspect of intuition strengthens as an individual's experience increases. In his book, *Outliers: The Story of Success*, Malcolm Gladwell explores research around the achievement of mastery—namely, the idea that it takes 10,000 hours to develop to a standard of "expert performance." (Just a note that more recent research has explored this claim in greater complexity, arguing that there are many additional variables that also impact our ability to achieve expert performance, including receiving consistent, expert feedback and the level of the individual's intelligence and memory.)

Although some would argue that this proves there is no such thing as intuition—only expertise—we believe this is just one aspect of a much more complicated system.

2) Mirror Neurons. Another key part of our intuition system is our ability to understand one another via mirror neurons. Mirror neurons fire both when an animal acts and when the animal observes the same action performed by another, an action with an intention behind it (it doesn't work with random, chaotic actions). Thus, the neuron "mirrors" the behavior of the other, as though the observer themselves were acting. For example, if someone takes a coffee cup and lifts it to their mouth to take a sip, an observer's mirror neurons will fire because the action can be understood as intentionally drinking. However, if the same observer simply waves the coffee cup around, no mirror neurons will fire, because it's not clear what the intention actually is.

Discovered in the 1990s, the function and extent of mirror neurons is still the subject of much speculation and debate. However, many researchers believe that the mirror neuron systems in the human brain *may* serve as the neural basis of emotions such as empathy and intuition, and are critical to our ability to learn from each other.

Mirror neurons function below conscious processing. In other words, we aren't generally aware that we're mirroring someone else, nor is it volitional. We see our friend about to bump his head on a doorway, and we instinctually duck ourselves. We watch someone eating a luscious piece of gooey chocolate cake on television and our own mouths water. These neurons fire quickly, providing information that might help us understand others' actions and intentions.

Often, we also physically mirror things we aren't consciously aware of, such as a fleeting body posture, a subtle tone of voice or even micro-movements in the face. All of this also provides information for our intuition system.

What is happening can occur so quickly we can't make any conscious sense of it, but our mirror neurons are tracking right along, cueing our own biochemistry to respond. This gives us that below-conscious-processing "gut" feeling or "hard-to-put-a-finger-on" sense of rightness or wrongness. Which brings us to…

3) The Vagus Nerve (and the body brain). From the Latin for "vague" or "wandering," the vagus nerve has branches that connect to most of the body's major organs. It conveys information about the body's state to the central nervous system: In fact, 80 to 90 percent of information traveling along the vagus nerve is flowing from the body to the brain, instead of vice versa. There are neurons in our heart and in our gut, and the information they gather flows back to the brain through the vagus nerve. Nearly every substance that helps run and control the brain has turned up in the gut, including major neurotransmitters like serotonin, dopamine, glutamate, norepinephrine and nitric oxide. The heart contains a well-developed independent nervous system with over 40,000 neurons and a complex and dense network of neurotransmitters, proteins and support cells. Thanks to these very elaborate circuits, it seems that the heart can make decisions and take action independently of the brain, and can learn, remember and even perceive. (It should come as no surprise that so many languages contain phrases that relate knowledge to the physical body, from having "a gut instinct" to learning something "by heart.")

We can intentionally access this part of the intuition system by checking in on our own physical reactions and body sensations—this includes the information we are picking up about others through our own mirror neurons.

It's also possible to strengthen the vagus nerve by increasing our capacity for "interoception," which is the awareness of our internal physical state. Sending a sort of antenna or feeler down our core from throat to gut and simply noticing the sensations there literally develops this key player in our intuition system. (The vagus nerve is also critical to emotional regulation, so doing this practice of interoception is very helpful in terms of becoming calmer and more able to recover when upset as well.)

4) The Right Hemisphere and the Default Mode Network.
Some information from our body comes into this side of our

brain through the Right Vagus Nerve. And while the right hemisphere is connected to many aspects of meaning and understanding, it does not have access to symbolic language and linear processes, largely the domain of the left hemisphere. The language of the right hemisphere is images, music, colors, emotions and metaphor. It's vague, unfocused, imprecise and broad. Thus it's up to us to take these amorphous feelings, images and "gut reactions" and find a way to talk about and understand them. When we say, "I have a *sense* of something, but I don't know how to describe it," we actually may be saying, "I have knowing in my right hemisphere, but I have not yet brought it into my left hemisphere through language so that it can be looked at specifically."

Using metaphor to get at our deeper knowing can be particularly helpful, in that it plays to the strengths of both hemispheres, from the vague sense or something that converts to an image, which then is described and sorted through language.

Another reason that there has been a tendency to label some people as intuitive and others as not is that our Default Mode Network (discussed in Chapter Four) also tends to provide meaning, interesting connections, insight, and "aha's." Tuning in to this network requires a relaxed, calm and open mind. Focus, drive, and analysis (more associated with the Task Positive Network) are a very different brain state, one in which this softer connection gets lost.

5) Our Senses. We have all heard that dogs can smell fear. In fact, humans can as well. As we noted in Chapter Three, studies ranging from the US Department of Defense to more than one major university in the US and Europe have found that we react to fear-induced sweat differently than exercise-induced sweat, even when it is not possible to actively identify a difference in odor.

Through smell, our own bodies experience the emotions of those around us, usually without any awareness. It's rare to use this as a conscious tool, although again, we use smell and other senses as metaphors for knowing, saying things like "it just doesn't smell right," or "that conversation left a bad taste in my mouth." And some people do seem to have particular gifts in this area. One of our friends recently mentioned that she knows what is going on with her teenagers based on how they smell. And perhaps we all have the capacity to use this skill more consciously. For example, we are often aware that we are attracted or repelled by someone's scent.

In addition to smell, other senses play into intuition in subtle, below conscious processing ways. For example, we may hear small tonal variations in someone's voice and just *know* something is wrong. (By the way, the ability to hear more subtlety in tone is linked to having a well-developed vagus nerve, which controls the muscles of the inner ear.) We may see something "off" and not even be fully aware we saw it, but again, just *know* something isn't as it should be. Even taste and touch can be part of this system, bringing in key information that may not be understood by the rational brain.

6) The Collective Consciousness. Any discussion of the intuition system would be incomplete without at least a nod to those things that we sometimes know are not in any way related to other aspects of the system. In other words, what we have no business knowing by any explainable means. Many people have some sort of example of this kind of intuition from thinking of someone just before that person calls to having a sense of foreboding about a trip.

Sometimes this happens when people are emotionally particularly close. Ann experienced a remarkable set of connections with her business partner and closest friend a few years ago when she was living in Costa Rica and her partner was in Florida. "Ursula called me one day to tell me she had woken up with a strange eye infection in her right eye. I had just that moment come home from a trip to the clinic where I had been diagnosed with a bad eye infection in my right eye. Another time, I woke up and couldn't move my shoulder without a great deal of pain. Ursula called me later that day and told me she had torn her rotator cuff."

This sort of connection and knowing is not actually that unusual. In fact, it is common enough that the United States Central Intelligence Agency has devoted millions of dollars studying various aspects of psychic phenomenon and has concluded that some rare individuals can indeed "read minds." And scientist Rupert Sheldrake, in his exploration of "morphic fields," has shown over and over that there are forces outside our immediate understanding. (Part of his research is the fascinating work on psychic bonds between animals and their owners.)

Many factors seem to contribute to a mastery of this area of intuition, but perhaps the most important is a calm, peaceful mind. Just as is the case with accessing our Default Mode Network, stress and busy-ness shut down what seems to be an innate and perhaps even universal ability to reach into the collective consciousness and "know."

Thus we would argue that intuition is a system, made up of at least six (if not more) interrelated aspects. As we have explained this and talked with people about it, we have found that everyone recognizes strengths and weaknesses in their own system. Understanding the systemic nature of intuition seems to help people value it and learn to develop their own innate abilities more fully.

The context of intuition helps us integrate ourselves by releasing our attachment to what we know (and can prove) strictly through conscious analysis to become larger, more expansive, and in effect, use more of our brains. It also expands our capacity for integration with others as we recognize that everything is not always apparent on the surface, or fixed and fixable. Intuition offers us a way to know the fullness of what's really going on, with ourselves, with others, with our world.

Einstein, it was said, was deeply intuitive, as was the prolific 19th and early 20th century inventor Nikola Tesla, and arguably, every great innovator we admire. Without intuition, there is little room for the broader conversation or for reaching into what's possible. Less of everything is available and life feels flat, stale and one-dimensional. When we bring intuition to the conversation, it becomes interesting, lively, multidimensional and deeply human.

The key with the context of intuition is that this kind of knowing—as powerful as it is—is imprecise. Thus, it is important to hold it lightly. In training, Co-Active coaches learn to recognize intuitive information and take a chance with it. They discover that their intuition is incredibly valuable for the coaching conversation, even if their own *interpretation* of what it means may or may not be accurate for the client. They are encouraged to offer what they are sensing without attachment, asking the client what, if anything, it might mean in the client's life or situation. In other words, they are trained to access the contexts of Curiosity and Self-Management in order to use their intuition most effectively.

Key Points

- Intuition is normal, rational, accessible and available to everyone.
- Intuition is yet another way of integrating different aspects and areas of our brains. It calls us to let go of what we know in order to know more.

- Intuitive information is everywhere—by understanding it as a system we can learn to both trust and expand our various information channels.

The Third Context—Curiosity

I think, at a child's birth, if a mother could ask a fairy godmother to endow it with the most useful gift, that gift should be curiosity.
~Eleanor Roosevelt

The next context is *Curiosity*, the space of not knowing, of staying open and being non-judgmental. This context calls for embracing a fascination with everything, a way of being with each other as sponges of observation and learning. This is somewhat countercultural in the West, as rewards tend to come to us for knowing and certainty, not for what the German poet Rainer Rilke called the ability to "live the question."

Without curiosity about ourselves and each other, we are limited and alone. If someone is not curious about you, it's like you're not really there for them, not a full, living breathing human being. As Oprah Winfrey said on the famous final episode of her long-running talk show, *"I've talked to nearly 30,000 people on this show, and all 30,000 had one thing in common—they all wanted validation... They want to know, do you hear me? Do you see me? Does what I say mean anything to you?"*

Human beings are complex, diverse, and unique. How can we know someone—really know them—if we think we have them all figured out before they even open their mouths? The paradox is, if you're not curious, not fully present with another, well, then they're not really there either. Nobody's home. The interaction has gone on autopilot.

Contrast this with the delicious interactions we have when we authentically want to know, want to explore, want to understand. Think about being on a first date, or perhaps having the chance to interview someone fascinating and unusual. There is often the experience of being in a sort of bubble of connection, where time ceases to have meaning and everything they say brings up multiple new questions. People often describe this as a "flow" state, and it simply isn't possible without curiosity.

That having been said, it's normal to not be curious about *everything*, and sometimes it's even helpful. The human brain is designed to move things into assumptions as a way of conserving energy. And it makes sense. We can generally assume the refrigerator is running when it is plugged in and therefore we don't need to waste energy worrying about whether or not our food is safe. We can assume that we will continue to receive payment for our work and therefore don't waste energy stressing about whether the rent or mortgage will be paid. We tend to assume our partner will continue to love us and don't need to obsess that each little mistake we make is the end of the relationship.

In each of these instances, we can easily imagine the opposite, and can see that if there were a power outage or erratic power surges, we would expend energy worrying about our frozen food. Or if our company were in a shaky financial situation, we would be very focused on wondering about our paycheck and ongoing security. Not to mention if things were not going well with our partner, we might become more inclined to stress about smaller things than we usually were. When we can't assume it simply takes energy, and our brains have an energy conservation default setting.

In many cases operating from some level of assumption helps us lead a more peaceful life. We don't want to go through our days wondering about our refrigerators, paychecks and partners, and those people who do may in fact have a brain pattern (for example, obsessive-compulsive disorder) which can profoundly disrupt their lives.

Neuroscience is showing us the critical importance of curiosity, however. Research using fMRI scans shows enhanced activity in brain areas associated with learning and behavioral change when the person is dealt with in an open, compassionate way. This activity is not present when the focus is on a person's failings and an answer is provided for them, which is all too often the way we deal with each other, our children, our employees or coworkers, etc. It's largely a default setting in many of our interactions, and we notice in our coach training that one of the most difficult things for many new Co-Active coaches is to let go of knowing, of having the answer, and simply become curious. For many of us, not knowing calls us out of a well-developed comfort zone.

Curious, powerful, open-ended questions have the impact of making us think and not just go onto autopilot. They engage our higher brains, including the prefrontal cortex, moving us out of the lower brain (which uses less energy) and into a place where reflection and inspiration become possible. This helps to anchor in learning, develop new neural pathways, and produce lasting growth.

Recent research at the University of California, Davis, has also shown that curiosity triggers dopamine, one of the reward chemicals in the brain, and this in turn stimulates memory. "There are times when people feel they can take in a lot of new information, and other times when they feel their memories are terrible," said Charan Ranganath, one of the study's authors. "This work suggests that once you light that fire of curiosity, you put the brain in a state that's more conducive to learning. Once you get this ramp-up of dopamine, the brain becomes more like a sponge that's ready to soak up whatever is happening."

Curiosity requires openness and a willingness to step into the unknown, which we might think of as being more the domain of the right hemisphere of the brain (judgment, certainty and closure being much more on the left). This is perhaps one of the reasons curiosity is not more prevalent in the Western world today. We tend to be rewarded for a left hemisphere view of things, with its tempting—though flawed and incomplete— tendency to certainty and absolutes. Contrast this with the way the right hemisphere experiences the world: as messy, unsure, complex and emergent. It takes patience to approach the world with curiosity at the slower pace of the right hemisphere, and we all too often simply don't take the time to do so.

So what role does curiosity play in the process of integration—the linkage of differentiated parts? Curiosity is deeply implicated in the process of differentiation, which is, as we have seen, crucial to linkage. If we are not curious about ourselves, others and the world, we can't find and know the parts we want to link.

Bernadetta was an example of this. A talented coach, she was in demand and very busy, and when asked how things were going, she'd smile and say, "It's all good!" But when she turned 50 she went on a yoga and meditation retreat in Spain. In that stillness, she found herself wondering if she was really happy. "I was meditating and the question sort of bubbled to the surface. I was surprised by how emotional I became as I realized I didn't know how to answer it. I loved my busy life, but it seemed there was something else my heart wanted as well." Bernadetta spent the next five days being curious about what happiness really meant to her. "By the end of the retreat, I realized I actually wanted it all. I didn't want to stop what I was doing, but I also wanted more space, more time like I had in Spain. So I went home and began a messy and imperfect process of new discovery. I'm still learning what my balance point is, but I am definitely happier now. And if you had asked me before Spain if I was happy, I would have said I couldn't be any happier!"

By being curious, Bernadetta discovered more differentiation within herself: the need for peace and stillness *and* engagement and busy-ness She was then able to work towards linking these elements, thus leading to far more integration (and resulting happiness) in her life.

Curiosity is also key in our ability to integrate with each other. When we think we already "know" who someone is, when we operate from assumptions rather than curiosity, we can't link with the real person in front of us. When we try to connect with who we *think* they are, nothing really sticks.

The truth is, we change all the time. In the play *Man and Superman* by George Bernard Shaw, the character Jack has this to say of how he was treated as he grew from boy to man: "The only person who behaved sensibly was my tailor. He took my measure anew each time he saw me." In other words, the tailor was the only person in his life who was curious and didn't assume.

There is an honoring of each other when we bring our full curiosity to the relationship. This isn't always easy, and it also creates some paradox. Part of the delight of long-term relationships is how well we know and are known. And yet, powerful relationships also allow for ongoing curiosity. For example, Ben and George have been business partners for many years, traveling the world consulting and training. They know what each other likes to eat, how much relaxation time the other needs, and what each brings in terms of strengths and weaknesses. They often finish each other's sentences and are known for the give and take in their connection.

"Still," Ben says, "we don't take each other for granted. And a big part of this is that we've learned to stay curious about the important things. Unless George tells me he's changing his diet, I know we're going for steak the first night we're on a trip. But what he thinks of a difficult client, or what new idea is turning in his head—that's another story. He never fails to fascinate me in terms of how his brain works, and I'm lucky that he seems to feel the same way about me. I know curiosity is a key part of our effectiveness with our clients. We are constantly turning everything over to see what might be there and what we can learn. After ten years of spending as much time with this guy as I probably do with my wife, I never get bored with him, and I never stop learning about him and from him."

Curiosity brings color to our life. Remember the Harry Chapin song about the young boy who goes to school and is corrected for drawing things the wrong way? "Flowers are red, young man," the teacher tells him. "And green leaves are green." The boy replies, "There are so many colors in the rainbow, so many colors in the morning sun. So many flowers in the garden, and I see every one." But he learns to please the teacher, and do things "the way they always have been done." Later, he meets a new teacher, who encourages him to break free and express himself again.

It's magical when we meet those who help restore our curiosity, and with it an innate and powerful sense of wonder. Curiosity helps us uncover the color and expression of a fulfilling life.

Key Points

- Curiosity opens up worlds within ourselves and others.
- It is the opposite of judgment, and a shortcut to authentic communication.
- Curiosity is natural. We don't learn to be curious—we learn *not* to be.
- We shut down curiosity in order to appear sophisticated and discerning.
- We have a natural brain inclination to move things into habit, and we definitely need to do so in many areas. This means living a truly conscious life can be a delicate balance.
- Curiosity is its own habit and gets easier the more we do it.

The Fourth Context—Forward the Action/Deepen the Learning

The act of calculating and getting answers is not a reflective activity... it does not generate understanding.
~James Zull

The fourth context is *Forward and Deepen*, the commitment to moving things *forward* while we also *deepen* our learning. This context reminds us that we are human *beings*, not human *doings*, and yet at the same time we all long for accomplishment and movement in our lives. You might say this is the height of integration, in that it honors both stillness and motion, pondering and achievement, "co" and "active."

Embracing this context gives dimension and meaning to our lives. On the one hand, if we just learn and don't apply, we can't lock in and make meaning of what we've learned. The learning makes no contribution because it is not engaged with our lives. When we don't use our learning, it is just data and doesn't touch or shape our lives.

On the other hand, if we just do-do-do, never stopping to reflect, we're just moving through the world with no growth or higher purpose. We may get a lot "done," but for the sake of what? We can't possibly become more effective without integrating the lessons available in our actions.

In order to change and become more integrated, we need both learning *and* action, and it doesn't matter where we start in the dance. We might start with an action, then reflect on its meaning, then use this awareness to take another action and so on. Or we might spend some time in reflection, from which an action arises. Then we might try that action, pause to reflect again, and so on. It makes no difference which comes first; the combination of the two becomes a virtuous cycle of learning, growth and accomplishment.

This is a place where we sometimes encounter some "either/ or" polarity thinking. For example, academia has traditionally valued the learning side, without as much emphasis on application. Ann recalls speaking with her undergraduate advisor about what do with her philosophy degree. "He looked at me like I had two heads when I told him I wanted to apply the principles I had been learning in the world somehow. I was astonished when he asked me, why would you want to do *that*? I told him I thought philosophy had great potential to help people and he told me this was not the point of the discipline. The point was, to discover truth. That's it."

Then there is the corporate world, where the focus is on doing, doing, doing. More! Better! Faster! It's not uncommon for people in many companies to run from meeting to meeting all day long, only able to catch up on e-mails and paperwork when they are at home in the evenings. There are many reasons this kind of culture isn't effective, including the fact that it allows little time for reflection or learning. Thus, people and organizations run the risk of making the same mistakes over and over again, dramatically reducing efficiency.

The context of Forward the Action/Deepen the Learning helps us balance between the extremes of processing endlessly versus moving from one thing to the next as if life were an assembly line. Instead it points us towards integration: doing things that move our lives forward *while also* reflecting and making meaning of what we have attempted and accomplished.

According to biology professor James Zull, there is a positive upward cycle of learning in the brain. Zull explains that when we *act*, our motor cortex carries out the plan of action. When we *recall* the experience, the sensory cortex receives the input from the five senses, and when we *reflect*, the back integrative cortex makes sense of the input. The frontal cortex (in charge of strategic thinking and planning) then uses the information from the back integrative cortex (which plays a role in locking in memory and reassembling sensory data) to develop or revise a plan of action for going forward.

To leave any of these steps out cheats us of potential development and growth, thus the critical importance of this context to our development and overall effectiveness. Additionally, holding the commitment to forward and deepen is important personally, in our one to one relationships, and with groups and organizations.

Laurie is a wonderful example of this. She spent endless hours thinking about and researching options and markets for her new coaching practice, finding it almost impossible to nail anything down. In working with her own coach, she realized that more thinking (as tempting as it was) was not going to get her anywhere on its own. So she began to try different things, bringing her experiences back to her coach for dissection and analysis.

In the process of trying out working with job seekers, students, and people wanting a change in their health, she found out much more about what she truly cared about. "I never would have realized my niche if I hadn't gotten out and tried," she reflected. "It simply wasn't possible to think it all through on its own, but as I worked with different people, I noticed where my energy was highest, and realized I don't care so much about *who* I coach. What I care about is *how* I do it." Laurie now "takes it to the streets" as a walking coach, which fits her passion for health and her own high energy. She also finds that when coach and client walk, new creativity and understanding emerge.

Even with the best of intentions, it's very easy to get caught up in the mode of do-do-do in today's fast-paced Western world. Ann has found this with her own business partner, Ursula. "Like many people, we're really good at action and moving things forward, but when we forget to stop and reflect, it's like the heart goes out of the enterprise. So we've developed a habit over the years of looking back in celebration on a regular basis to see where we've come and what we've learned. It's so easy to focus forward—there is always a next critically important thing to do. And when we also stop and look back, it gives us information and energy to continue on. We've learned it doesn't have to be a big thing—even playing the 'remember when' game is often enough, as long as we also noodle around with what we learned and where we've come to as a result."

Key Points

- When we forward the action and deepen the learning, it is the height of integration. This is true within ourselves, with each other, and in the greater world.
- Each aspect needs the other, and there is no right place to start. Start somewhere—action will lead to learning, and learning to action.
- Forward the Action/Deepen the Learning lifts us out of polarity thinking and makes room for the possibility that there is a gift in everything.
- Everything that happens is an opportunity to learn and grow. No matter what happens, there is learning possible and that learning can inform action. This takes us out of victim thinking, which is key to development.

The Fifth Context—Self-Management

The emotional brain responds to an event more quickly than the thinking brain.
~Daniel Goleman

The final context is *Self-Management*. As we saw in the discussion above about Level One listening, it is natural for human beings to relate to others' experiences through their own filters. In fact, if someone tells us they are working on an exciting new project to "maxiloop" the performance appraisal process in their company, we would probably give them a blank stare (or tune out all together). But if they stop and say, "Oh, sorry, in our company we have this funny word for maximizing the connections between groups," we can connect and relate. This is because subconsciously, without any effort or intention, we've gone into our own experience with "maxilooping" and therefore are able to sense what it might be like.

This is, of course, where Self-Management comes in. Without Self-Management—the capacity to set aside our own biases and reactions—it's difficult to move our listening to Levels Two and Three, remain curious, and use intuition for the sake of learning and growth.

There is an important distinction needed here, which is that Self-Management is different than suppression. Shutting down how we really feel, "going along to get along," etc, are all fear-based strategies. Self-Management is the ability to notice our own Level One and emotional reactions, and choose what to use or share for the sake of the relationship, the designed alliance, and the stake.

Because we are so programmed to understand each other through our own experiences, this context is absolutely critical. We can learn to distinguish our own Level One listening, use it for information, but ultimately put the focus back on another person or group.

Self-Management is not just something we need in relationship with each other; it's also an important key in terms of our relationship with ourselves. We need the capacity to manage our own very quick "emotional brains" not only when someone else provides a trigger, but also in terms of our Level One listening within and about ourselves—Self-Management helps us stay open and curious about our own patterns and habitual reactions.

When we look at Self-Management from the perspective of integration, we see that it helps us to *differentiate* our own experience, understanding what parts are informative and helpful in the situation or relationship, leaving out the rest. And then, we are able to *link* with others by bringing in only what is most helpful (self-managing to leave the rest behind). If we think back to the Designed Alliance (the shoreline of our lake), self-management gives us the agility to bring different parts of ourselves forth in service of the alliance, in service of the stake.

The more of yourself you can access and bring forward, the

more effective you can be in a wide range of situations. For example, Luis is a business leader, a warm and friendly person with a natural gift for seeing possibilities. However, he realized at one point in his career that his passion sometimes made him run off at the mouth. "I used to have a problem getting carried away with myself. I would talk and talk and talk about my vision and never notice that people's eyes were glazing over." He wondered why he wasn't able to infuse others with his enthusiasm, and often blamed them for lacking imagination.

In a leadership program, he became aware that his energy could be overwhelming to some people. "I began doing a better job of managing my impact," he reported. "I used to think I had to share *everything* so that people would understand a project on the level that I did. And I thought if they understood it like me, they would jump in a thousand percent. I could never figure out why they didn't!" Luis learned the important lesson of "less is more" in his sharing, and in the process also saw that, in the act of talking, he had not been listening. "I was often so excited there was simply no space for anyone else. Someone told me, 'I really love and respect you, Luis, but you have a way of taking up all the air in the room.' That was one of those life-changing moments. I didn't want to hear it, but it was true. When I slowed down, gave more space, I learned a lot."

Luis found Self-Management critical to his ability to have integration with others, as well as with himself. There was not only room for other ideas and enthusiasm, his own understanding of his vision went even deeper and he was far more at peace with himself.

In a group, when people are practicing Self-Management, there is an overall sense of emotional intelligence and a palpable feeling that things can be moved forward easily and effectively. As we have explored elsewhere in this book, we have a very strong tendency towards "fight or flight," and according to neuroscience research, one of the things that can really set us off is the feeling that our status has been threatened. (Brain imaging technology has even found that the pain of social rejection is felt in places in the brain that are very near to the places we feel physical pain. Being left out hurts.)

It's easy to see why Self-Management would be so crucial to the high functioning of a group. The skill of noticing emotional reactions, and then choosing a response rather than reacting is key to a truly high-functioning, healthy team. For example, being challenged in a meeting can initially feel like a threat and a potential loss of status. But if, instead of reacting, we take a deep breath and stay present and curious by self-managing our immediate emotional reaction, something more productive may occur. The same is true if we are the challenger. Self-Management, being aware of our defaults and again, staying present, may help us to say things in a more open and engaging manner and tone. This keeps connection, relationship and, ultimately, productivity intact.

A leader and a group who are aware of Self-Management can create the kind of relationship where roles move fluidly around the group and there is an ease and flow of communication. Sandra is a great example of this. She read *The Four Agreements* by Don Miguel Ruiz and was struck by the importance of one of the agreements: not taking things personally. "I immediately saw how much I did this (took things personally) without thinking. And then, of course, I noticed it in everyone around me as well. As a leader, I saw that people on my team were reacting to things that often were in no way meant to be about them. So I brought in the idea that maybe things weren't as personal as we were often making them. I had to kind of harp on it at first, but it worked. After I had said 'hold on, let's just look at this impersonally' enough, I noticed that people started to do it on their own. Meetings calmed down and there were fewer 'water cooler' conversations. You know, the meeting after the meeting!" Sandra helped her team self-manage their own reactions and stay more present to the bigger issue and purpose, thus increasing their overall effectiveness.

Key Points

- Self-Management helps us choose with discernment the part of ourselves which is best to have in the driver's seat at any given time.
- It helps us managing reactive tendencies—both within ourselves or with others.
- Self-Management is critical to the other contexts.
- It's important to know the point or the stake that you are self-managing around or for.

How the waters merge

A lake carries you into recesses of feeling otherwise impenetrable.
~William Wordsworth

And so, in looking at these five keys to integration, we have navigated the waters of the Co-Active lake:

- **Listening** opens our *presence*;
- **Intuition** opens our *knowing* and is about *accessing* other streams of information;
- **Curiosity** opens our *experience*;
- **Forward the Action/Deepen the Learning** opens up *meaning* and *application*; and
- **Self-Management** opens our *effectiveness* and is critical to all other contexts.

Perhaps, as we have moved from one context to another, we've noticed that rather than being clear and distinct, they meld and merge together:

- True **Listening** requires self-management, curiosity, access to intuition, as well as being able to hear when it is time to forward the action and when it is time to deepen the learning.
- **Intuition** occurs in the higher levels of listening, piques our curiosity, gives us cues about action and learning, and requires self-management as we share it with others, offering, not dictating.
- **Curiosity** takes us to Level Two and Three listening, dances with intuition, has us check out whether action or learning is needed, and is our best tool for self-management.
- **Forward the Action/Deepen the Learning** uses authentic listening and intuition to know what is needed, tapping into curiosity about what learning or action is helpful next.
- **Self-Management** is augmented by a commitment to listening at Levels Two and Three, which makes it more difficult to take things personally, using our deeper intuition to stay present and aware, being curious rather than shutting down and reacting, and always looking for what is of greatest benefit for self or group—forwarding the action, or deepening the learning.

Words cannot begin to capture reality.
Here, I've written some words about reality.
Oh, the gorgeous paradox.
~Jeff Foster

Conclusion

Human cultures progress through a dance of specialization and integration.

~Earon Davis

Ann's story, revisited

One of the gifts of losing my hair is that it made me uncomfortably and unavoidably aware of separation/interconnectedness as the primary human challenge. But that awareness wasn't the answer in and of itself—it was more like a signpost pointing the way back home to the truest possibility of who we can be.

Discovering the Co-Active model thirteen years ago has been a key part of this journey. Like many who take these innovative coaching courses, I ended up using a number of tools and concepts from the model without even necessarily being aware of it. For example, about ten years ago I decided to experiment with not wearing a wig. In doing so, I needed to hold myself (in the words of the Co-Active model) not only as naturally creative, resourceful, and whole, but also very much as a whole person, even though I didn't look like everyone else.

My experiment lasted about five years, and in that time I learned volumes about human compassion and connection. I had endless conversations at checkout counters, in line at the bank, on airplanes— always because someone assumed I had cancer. At first, to be honest, I was profoundly irritated. But after a while (I think because I came to understand these conversations were inevitable), I realized that people only wanted to connect, and my hair loss gave them the opening they were hungry for.

When I began to view others not simply as intruders but whole people as well, it became clear that they were eager to tell me their stories and provide encouragement. "Look at me, I'm two years, cancer-free," they'd say. "You can do it!" Or they'd tell me I still looked beautiful, or that it gets better, or simply that they understood. Nothing could have more deeply reflected to me (even as I assured them I was fine) the depth of human longing to reach one another.

So, over the past 30-odd years, I can honestly say that I've walked the path as best I can. Have I arrived? I don't think so, but I know I'm getting closer, and in the process learning to honor the paradox of discovering (and becoming more fully) who I am at my core, while artfully connecting with others and experiencing the synergy and beauty of co-creation.

Karen's story, revisited

At the beginning of this book, I say that my battle with Bulimia was my salvation, and these words are so true. The path to healing and recovery has been a journey into self-authority and self-love. I've learned how to embrace my own (and others') differences, holding them as fertile ground to make life more interesting rather than problems to be solved.

In many ways, the pain of my adolescent sense of isolation provided the raw material from which I was able to help create a model of wholeness, inclusion and integration. My own journey provided a much larger context in which to hold the humanity of both myself and others, and this was crucial in helping to birth CTI and the Co-Active Way.

As I travel the world, many people tell me that CTI has changed their lives. I know what they are talking about, because it's true for me as well. In practicing the tools and embracing the mindset of being Co-Active, I have continued to grow as a partner, a leader, and a human being. It has been a complete joy to give myself to the work of the Co-Active Model and the ongoing co-creation of CTI, in the process growing more confident and becoming very clear about why I am here in this lifetime.

Self-knowledge is an ongoing exploration and adventure, and these days I can honestly say that I am both comfortable with and curious about the unique expression that is Karen Kimsey-House. I have a true sense of my strengths and can hold huge compassion for the places I still need to grow and change.

As I look back over the tapestry of my life, I see that every single thing that occurred, every challenge, every hardship, every victory and every decision has been a contribution. Were I to have designed a program to prepare me for the work I do today, I could not have done a better job, even though much of it didn't always make sense at the time. I'm sure there were many occasions when my parents wondered if I would ever get my act together. There were many times I wondered this myself. And yet, as I reflect back, there was a masterful design to all of it.

Most importantly, I can say that I am comfortable in my own skin. I am a robust and healthy woman. I dress as I please and care for myself in ways that make sense to me. I haven't thought about dieting for ages. Most of the time, I am present to the joy of each moment. I have learned to empower and pay attention to what brings me joy and pleasure, and turn away from that which is not life affirming.

Certainly I am not perfect and my life is not perfect. Recently, I watched a video of myself and had a sudden "shame attack." The self-judgment came flooding in, which surprised me as I had not experienced that kind of shame for a long time. But now, I have tools to recover, and was able to do that pretty quickly. It was a wonderful reminder that we are all works in progress, and the point is not perfection, but to stay in the game, continuing to explore, feel, process and integrate.

I feel broadly loved and am so grateful for the many people that I have come to know intimately over these past years. That said, the love I cherish the most is that which I am able to direct towards myself, and I hope to continue nourishing that flame of the heart for many years to come.

Throughout this book we've experienced a journey of integration—an exploration of our Co and our Active, our need to both be and do, our masculine and feminine nature, and how different parts of our brain function and interact. A journey towards greater wholeness, within ourselves and our relationships, which ultimately impacts the world.

We don't need to pursue integration in order to get by in life. We can hang out in our comfort zones on one side of a polarity or the other. In doing so, however, we can spend precious time and life energy arguing for the side we hold as right, proper or the "only" way.

But why? Why settle for half a life, when so much more is available?

The only argument we can see is that it's not always easy. If it were, we'd all be nicely integrated already. Human beings are complex and multifaceted, relationships and organizations even more so, and societies the most complex of all. Given all these parts, pieces, competing ideas and energies, the process of creating a greater sense of integration simply within ourselves alone represents a formidable challenge—one we feel, however, is of vital importance and well worth the effort indeed.

We've emphasized that integration is essential for our species to evolve and grow to the next level. The world is becoming increasingly complex, challenging, and paradoxical. Little is black and white any more, and many become overwhelmed because they don't have sufficient tools or self-awareness. We need to develop sophistication in how we both think and act to be able to move effectively, rather than just being run over by our complex world. We desperately need to become more integrated in order to traverse the ever-present grey areas we increasingly encounter in our lives.

What would be different in our world if we were able to hold and navigate this level of complexity, to foster both the being and the doing, the *Co* and the *Active*? What would be different if all of our actions arose from a ground of meaning and purpose, if we were able to make the "why" even more important than the "what?" Einstein's well-known quote comes to mind: "The intuitive mind is a sacred gift and the rational mind a faithful servant." We certainly have, in the words of a commentator on this notion, "created a society that honors the servant and has forgotten the gift." What would be possible for all of us if this balance were restored?

And thus we believe that not only is pursuing integration essential, the good news is that the more we do so—individually and collectively—the easier it becomes. As we've mentioned, Rupert Sheldrake talks about the power of morphic resonance, the way self-organizing systems inherit a memory from previous similar systems, creating in the individual a collective memory from past members of the species. This individual in turn contributes to the collective memory, impacting other members of the species in the future. In other words, through our individual and collective efforts of integration, we help to pave the way for those to come.

The clarion call of our time is to build and strengthen the morphic field of integration—and it's a call we believe is already being heeded and is well underway. We are living in a time of change unprecedented in human history. Consider, for example, how education has changed in the past 50 years to a more collaborative model with less focus on sheer memorization and repetition. Or, the emerging conversation about mindfulness in the workplace. Consider how Wikipedia has created a platform for co-creative learning with unlimited experts and a self-regulating community. There are online forums on every possible topic, with ordinary people sharing stories and advice. The business world is rapidly becoming international in scope, with even small businesses successfully reaching customers across the world through the Internet. Likewise, the profession of coaching has reached global proportions, dedicated to helping people everywhere create more balance and fulfillment in their lives. The process of integration has begun and is unfolding before us.

There are many examples of success and movement toward integration, with equal numbers of failure and resistance. This reminds us of a well-known story about a man who encounters a butterfly half-emerged from its chrysalis. He watches it struggling and, overcome with pity, takes out his pocketknife and cuts it free of the shell. The butterfly stretches its wings in the sun, and the man sees that while one wing is perfectly developed, the other is small and withered. The poor butterfly is unable to fly. It needed to push against the chrysalis in order to strengthen its wings and emerge fully developed and ready for the world.

Thus we see that the birth of something new always involves struggle. And this is OK. The conversation has begun and will continue, and we've done our best to offer our collective voice in this book, creating a map for the journey as best we understand it today. More will emerge and unfold as we continue to evolve, and we understand the world may resist our efforts at times. This is all part of the natural process of evolution.

It's important to note that Co-Active is but one of many movements or efforts happening throughout the world today with the intent to foster integration, harmony and peace. We see the Co-Active way as being a part of the larger collaboration and orchestration of global change. We are not playing alone, and in this spirit of harmony we are accompanied by many others who are also committed to Joanna Macy's "Great Turning"—the shift away from disconnection and disharmony to a life-sustaining, fully integrated civilization.

There are now well over 40,000 people all over the world who have been touched by the Co-Active model. They are using its distinctions and tools as parents, managers, leaders, students, artists, partners, educators, individuals and life coaches. In doing so, they have experienced profound and lasting transformation in every area of life—often being a source of evoking transformation in the lives around them as well. We've shared a few of their stories here, and there are thousands more, guided by the map of integration the Co-Active model provides.

We've seen that when we use this map, we arrive at a place where we feel effective, hopeful, and profoundly satisfied. And there is much more to come, more vistas to explore, more mountains to climb.

Let's go.

When we reach a "critical mass" of integration, we experience spontaneous combustion—an explosion of inner synergy that ignites the fire within and gives vision, passion, and a spirit of adventure to life.

~Stephen Covey

Footnotes

1. The influential seventeenth century French philosopher René Descartes famously said: "I think, therefore I exist (cogito ergo sum)." He arrived at this conclusion by realizing he could doubt everything (he posited that his very existence and everything he encountered could be manufactured by what he calls a "deceiving God") except that fact that he doubted. His views were powerfully influential and propelled us into further separation from ourselves and each other as the left hemisphere capacity to analyze and reduce was seen as the ultimate triumph of knowledge and understanding.

2. "Integration in the brain... involves the linkage of differentiated neural areas and their specialized functions with each other. (This is done through focusing attention, which) directs the flow of energy and information through particular neural circuits." (Siegel 2010)

References

Chapter One

Andrews, Mark. "How does background noise affect our concentration?" *Scientific American*, January 2010

Brown, Brené. *I Thought It Was Just Me (but it isn't)*. Gotham, 2007

Bureau of Labor Statistics. "American Time Use Survey Summary." US Department of Labor, 2012

Herbert, Wray. "Rx for Sisyphus, take two Tylenol..." *Journal of Psychological Science*, September 2012

Land, George and Jarman, Beth. *Breakpoint and Beyond*. San Francisco: HarperBusiness, 1993

Mehl, Matthias. "Eavesdropping on Happiness: Well-being is Related to Having Less Small Talk and More Substantive Conversations." *Psychological Science*, February 2010

Walsch, Neale Donald. "The Importance of Separation." *Spirit Library*, November 2010

Chapter Two

Arnsten, Amy. "The Mental Sketchpad: Why Thinking has Limits." NeuroLeadership Summit Lecture, 2008

Bolte-Taylor, Jill. *My Stroke of Insight*. Viking, 2006

"'Doomsday Clock' Moves Two Minutes Closer to Midnight." Bulletin of the Atomic Scientists, 2007

Diamond, Jared. "The Worst Mistake in the History of the Human Race." *Discover Magazine*, May 1987

Dunbar, Robin IM. How Many Friends Does One Person Need?: Dunbar's Number and Other Evolutionary Quirks. Faber and Faber, 2010

Ladinksy, Daniel. *Love Poems From God*. Penguin, 2002

McGilchrist, Iain. *The Master and His Emissary: The Divided Brain and the Making of the Western World*. Yale University Press, 2009

Nelson, Craig. *Rocket Men*. Viking, 2009

Chapter Three

Bloom and Hynd. "The Role of the Corpus Callosum in Interhemispheric Transfer of Information: Excitation or Inhibition?" *Neuropsychology Review*, Vol. 15, No. 2, June 2005

Cuddy, Amy. "Your body language shapes who you are." *TEDGlobal*, June 2012

de Groot et al. "Chemosignals Communicate Human Emotions." *Journal of Psychological Science*, 2012

Gallup Consulting, www.gallup.com

Luders, Eileen; Clark, Kristi; Narr, Katherine; Toga, Arthur. "Enhanced Brain Connectivity in Long-term Meditation Practitioners." *NeuroImage*, 2011

Holt, Jim. "Of Two Minds." *New York Times*, May 2005

Rock, David. "SCARF: a brain-based model for collaborating with and influencing others," *NeuroLeadership Journal*, Issue One 2008

Siegel, Daniel. *Pocket Guide to Interpersonal Neurobiology*. New York: Norton, 2012

Chapter Four

Arbinger Institute. *The Anatomy of Peace*. Berrett-Koehler Publishers, 2006

Dutton, Kevin. "Wisdom from Psychopaths?" *Scientific American Mind*, Jan/Feb 2013

Chapter Five

Arnsten, Amy. "The Mental Sketchpad: Why Thinking has Limits." NeuroLeadership Summit Lecture, 2008

Boyatzis, Richard. "Neuroscience and the Link Between Inspirational Leadership and Resonant Relationships." Ivey Business Journal, Jan/Feb 2012

Bradley; McCraty; Tomasino. "The Resonant Heart." Institute of HeartMath, 2005

Doidge, Norman. *The Brain That Changes Itself*. Penguin Books, 2007

Jha, Amishi. "Being in the Now." *Scientific American Mind*, March/April 2013

Rock and Page. *Coaching with the Brain in Mind*. Wiley, 2009

Siegel, Daniel. *Pocket Guide to Interpersonal Neurobiology*. New York: Norton, 2012

Sterling Livingston, J. "Pygmalion in Management." *Harvard Business Review*, September/October 1988

Chapter Six

Harvey, Jerry B. *The Abilene Paradox and Other Meditations on Management*. Lexington Books, 1988

Chapter Seven

Anderson, Cameron et al. "The Local-Ladder Effect: Social Status and Subjective Well-Being." *Psychological Science*. 2012

Boyatzis, Richard and Jack, Anthony. "Coaching with compassion can 'light up' human thoughts." Case Western Reserve University, 2010

Creswell, JD; Welch, WT; Taylor, SE; Sherman, DK; Gruenewald, TL; and Mann, T. "Affirmation of personal values buffers neuroendocrine and psychological stress responses." Department of Psychology, University of California. Los Angeles, 2005

Gruber, Matthias; Gelman, Bernard; Ranganath, Charan. "States of Curiosity Modulate Hippocampus-Dependent Learning via the Dopaminergic Circuit." *Neuron*, October 2014

Lieberman, Matthew. *Social: Why Our Brains Are Wired to Connect*. Crown, 2013

Recker, Gary; Peacock, Edward; Wong, Paul. "Meaning and Purpose in Life and Well-Being." Oxford: *Journal of Gerontology*, Volume 42, Issue 1, 1985

Sheldrake, Rupert. http://www.sheldrake.org/research/morphic-resonance

Zull, James. *The Art of Changing the Brain*. Virginia: Stylus Publishing, 2002

About the Authors

Karen Kimsey-House, MFA, CPCC, MCC, Co-founder, CEO & Director, CTI, www.thecoaches.com
One of the earliest recognized luminaries in the coaching profession, Kimsey-House founded CTI in 1992 with Laura Whitworth and Henry Kimsey-House. They created the Co-Active philosophy of relationship that informs CTI's world-renowned coaching and leadership programs. She also is a blogger for *The Huffington Post* and the coauthor of *Co-Active Coaching*, the best-selling industry bible, now in its third edition. A successful entrepreneur, Kimsey-House received her MFA in Communications and Theater from Temple University in Philadelphia, PA. Committed to pioneering Co-Active tools and principles in challenged environments and troubled populations, Kimsey-House continues to lead CTI workshops and is a dynamic keynote speaker around the world. On a mission of global, transformative change, she lives with her husband, Henry Kimsey-House, by the Pacific Ocean.

Ann Betz, CPCC, Co-founder, BEabove Leadership, CTI Faculty and Neuroscience Consultant, www.beaboveleadership.com
Ann Betz, CPCC is the co-founder of BEabove Leadership, and an international speaker and trainer on the intersection of neuroscience, coaching, and human transformation. An ongoing student of the brain, Ann's studies include graduate work at the NeuroLeadership Institute and with Dan Siegel. She is on the faculty of the Coaches Training Institute and also serves as their neuroscience consultant. Ann is a popular author on coaching and the brain as a contributor to *Choice Magazine*, *Coaching at Work*, and other coaching and HR publications as well as her own blog at
www.yourcoachingbrain.wordpress.com.

Through BEabove Leadership, Ann developed and co-leads the popular training program for advanced coaches: *Neuroscience, Consciousness and Transformational Coaching*, currently available in the US, Canada and the UK. Ann delights audiences all over the world with her ability to make the complexities of the brain and consciousness accessible, relevant, and fun. She shares her home in Celebration, Florida with two very enlightened cats.